YOU TRY IT

DR. ROBERT A. RUSSELL

Audio Enlightenment Press

Giving Voice to the Wisdom of the Ages

Printed in the United States of America

First Printing, 2022
ISBN 978-1-941489-96-3

www.RobertARussell.Org

Table of Contents

Introduction 1

Part One 3

    Chapter I: Try Putting First Things First 5

    Chapter II: Try Facing the Wind 15

    Chapter III: Try Faith in Solving Problems 23

    Chapter IV: Try Faith in a Plan 31

    Chapter V: Try Faith in Action.. 41

    Chapter VI: Try Faith in Healing 49

    Chapter VII: Try Faith in Prosperity 71

    Chapter VIII: Try Making a Personal Check-Up 85

Part Two 101

    Chapter IX: Practicing the Presence of God 103

    Chapter X: Magnifying the Light... 123

    Chapter XI: Releasing the Real Self 145

    Chapter XII: Making an End of Praying 157

Introduction

We can inherit money, we can borrow another man's car, we can buy an artist's painting, we can enjoy the genius of the musician, we can utilize the skill of the designer, the architect, the conductor, the artisan. Every hour of the day, our lives are made easier, pleasanter, and more secure by the work of another man's brain and hand.

But we cannot buy or borrow or steal another person's belief — his religion or philosophy. We may admire it as we see it in action in his life, we may understand it mentally and sympathize with it emotionally, but it is not ours until it becomes an integral part of our experience through acceptance and realization. It is a thing apart until we have tried it for ourselves.

The difference between *mine* and *thine* dawns on us slowly. Most of us can remember the shock we had when we began to be aware of the distinction. Perhaps the experience occurred in the home and was associated with a material object such as a toy or piece of money. If the awakening came at school, it was in all probability attached to the teacher's insistence that we draw our own picture and not copy our neighbor's, or to the painful recovery that every one else seemed how to spell the word dictated or solve the problem given and that their knowledge didn't help us at all.

But it would be a strange and cruel world if we could profit only by our own experience. Sympathy, understanding, and generosity would be very limited. The instant response to disaster anywhere on the face of the globe is proof of man's ability to sense the experience of others. The degree of his understanding, however, is determined by the extent to which phases of the experience is similar to experiences of his own. In this day of motion pictures, radio, television, and abundant print, his concepts are greatly enlarged. But have you not many times said, or thought, or heard these words, "Nothing in my experience has prepared me for this," referring to a catastrophe such as a tornado, an epidemic, a fire, the loss of a dear one, or perhaps to sudden and unexpected success, to elevation to a high office, or to newly-acquired wealth?

There is abundant proof today of man's interest in religion. He wants to know what is happening to him and why, he is tired of feeling that he is a football of fate, he yearns for happiness, security, and strength. Increase in church attendance and membership is reported from every quarter. Radio broadcasts presenting many and varied forms of religion are common. Books on related subjects abound. The very fact that you are reading this page at this moment is proof that you are among those who realize that *"man cannot live by bread alone."*

Here within these covers you may find the help you are seeking. Read with an open mind but realize that reading is not to an end itself. Until you integrate your information with your experience, you do not KNOW. Put aside your doubts, your skepticism, your self-consciousness, and *"become as a little child."* Develop the equalities of faith and acceptance that are inherent and enter into the plane of realization.

You will know and so will those around you when you have found what you are looking for. The psychologist says that learning is that reorganization of experience and behavior. Jesus said, *"By their fruits ye shall know them."*

You try it.

Part One

Chapter I
Try Putting First Things First

Religion is entering upon a new day. A new demand is being made upon the church. New fires are breaking out in the heart of the congregation. New life is rushing in from hitherto unknown sources. New voices are speaking from another dimension.

The old shibboleths are falling apart because they are worn out. The fear and dread engendered by worship of a tribal God are now giving way to the peace and confidence that come from a recognition of eternal Truth — the Presence of the Indwelling God. The Heaven in the skies has come down to man in a state of harmonious consciousness. The imperious call of the ministry is no longer *"Prepare to meet thy God,"* but *"Acquaint now thyself with Him, and be at peace."* Man is learning that the Highest God and the Innermost God are one God and that he is one with Him.

It is not a new religion nor an abrogation of the old. Humanity's idea of the Old Testament God changed materially with the coming of Jesus, but throughout the centuries His words have lost their meaning for many. Today we interpret His sayings and read His promises literally. We accept the need to change our consciousness in order to enter His Kingdom, and we see that Kingdom not as a far-off place in the Heavens reached by climbing the golden stairs but as the peace secured by our recognition of and unification with the Father Within.

This religion is not a once-a-week affair; since the result in one's life is determined by the state of his consciousness, and one's consciousness is made of all that he is — all that he thinks, believes, feels, hopes, and does, religion becomes the one constant factor in the Truth student's life.

Humanity is now finding an interpretation of the gospels that works. The mirage has become an oasis. *"Look up, and lift up your heads for your redemption draweth nigh."*

In the old formal religion, the emphasis was upon saving man's soul. In practical religion, the emphasis is upon saving the whole man. In orthodoxy, the call was "Come to Jesus." In rational theology, the order is "Release the Christ." Read the Sermon on the Mount," and you will see, that Jesus was not exclusively interested in man's spiritual needs. He was concerned also with the common daily round of his material needs. Did He not heal the sick and feed the hungry? Did He not say that *"All things are yours"?* And do *things* not include clothes, food, health, and economic security?

"But you are forgetting," says the theologian, "that Jesus told man to *'Take no thought for the morrow.'* "

"You have missed His meaning," replies the metaphysician. " *'Take no thought'* does not mean to stop thinking about basic necessities, but to stop worrying about them. If you read the rest of the passage, you will see that, instead of minimizing these human wants, He is actually telling up how to demonstrate or materialize them. His message on the subject is very clear: *'Your heavenly Father knoweth that ye have need of all these things. But seek ye first the Kingdom of God and His righteousness; and all these things shall be added unto you.'* "

You do not get happiness, health, and prosperity by begging for them, by striving for them, or by pouncing upon them. They follow your fulfillment of a prior condition. Something else comes first. You may put your family, your friends, your business, social, or lodge life, first, but you will never get the things you most want until you have complied with the condition; that is seek *"first the Kingdom of God and His righteousness."*

The slogan, "America First," was on everybody's lips until the weakness in it became apparent. Of course, we want America to be a great leader and power in the world, but something else must come first. Without righteousness, American cannot stand. Without consideration of others, she cannot prosper. Without God, she cannot succeed.

The dictionary defines *righteousness* as a state or quality of being rightful. The Law of Righteousness is a basic law of metaphysical science; all spiritual blessings depend upon its practice. Put righteousness first, *"and all these things shall be added unto you"* — healing for your body, peace for your soul, prosperity in your affairs, and security for your family.

When a certain shoe manufacturer was asked the secret of his success, he pointed to a motto carved in oak on his office wall:

> GOD — FIRST
>
> FAMILY — SECOND
>
> SHOES — THIRD

How could anyone be a failure with a motto such as that?

We often put the wrong things first. We try to take the greater from the lesser. Does a man get the accessories before he purchases the car? Does a woman buy the drapes, carpets, and furniture before she secures the house? We work at cross-purpose with the Principle of Life when we spend our energy trying to get *things* and postpone the effort to establish the Kingdom. Material food does not satisfy a starving and impoverished soul. The man who puts money first finds that it doesn't buy happiness, health, or peace.

"Your heavenly Father knoweth that ye have need of all these things." What disillusionment and discouragement can come to those that forget the command that follows — the command to seek Him first!

Do you understand what it means to put righteousness first? It means to surrender your human mind and its thinking to the Mind of Christ. Jesus has made it clear that He wants you to have healing, wholeness, and financial security and that these things must come to you by His way of appointing. *"Of myself* [with the human mind] *I can do nothing." "The Father* [the Christ Mind] *that dwelleth in me, He doeth the works."*

Jesus did not say, "Take right thought for the morrow"; He said. *"Take no thought."* In other words, stop trying to solve problems and heal conditions for yourself. The personal self must be denied; it must be eliminated so that *"the Mind which was also in Christ Jesus"* can go to work.

Emerson said in forceful terms, "Get your bloated nothingness out of the way of the Divine Circuit."

The human mind, thinking always in terms of good and evil and not according to Principle, cannot know the Truth. Knowing both good and evil, it is unreliable and unstable. But the Spiritual Mind sees and knows and calls into being only the good.

The metaphysical definition of righteousness — the right use of the law — gives a clue to our problem. When we *"Know the*

Truth," the Mind of Christ becomes our mind. Then this Mind produces right action in all our affairs.

How do we enable the Mind of Christ to become our mind? By refusing to entertain human beliefs, fears, worries, thoughts, and preconceived opinions; by turning to God; by allowing the responsibility for knowing the Truth to rest not upon our shoulders but upon God's. Have you been trying to get God's attention? Then still your human mind and listen to these words: *"Before they call I will answer, and while they are yet speaking I will hear." "Your Father knoweth what things ye have need of before ye ask him."*

Pleading with God to solve a problem that is already solved is about as sensible as begging the ocean to float a ship. What is needed is intelligent cooperation with the Principle of Life. God is Causative Power which forever produces according to Law. To have the Mind of Christ is to have the Mind of God in action.

Whenever Jesus' disciples became disturbed or upset, He offered peace to them. To the raging sea, He said, *"Peace, be still."* To seek *"The Kingdom of God and His righteousness"* is to be spiritually minded. St. Paul tells us that *"to be spiritually minded is life and peace."*

Jesus did not come to build a lot of cults and religious organizations, but to instill a concept and to vitalize it. The concept is that of our immediate and continuous access to His wholeness and abundance, our endowment of power, and our ability to be whatever we desire to do. If we choose to be mediocre and second-rate, that choice is our own business. If we reject happiness and success, we can blame nobody but ourselves. The choice is up to the individual. The blessings that Christ offers are for those who are willing to follow the

Law of Righteousness and Truth. To get results, we must accept the responsibility of choosing.

"But I have a family to support, obligations to meet, conditions to be healed, and problems to be solved." you say, "and you tell me that I must put something else first." And I still insist that while your wants are important, there is a condition to be fulfilled before your needs can be met.

A cement man gives me a formula for concrete: so much sand, so much cement, and so much water. It is a formula that has never failed. But cement is high these days; sand is cheaper. I think to myself, "Maybe I can get along with a little less cement. I shall skimp on cement a bit." What happens? The concrete doesn't hot hold up. It crumbles away. The formula is tried and true, but I failed to follow it.

I have an urgent letter to send. I ought to send it by special delivery. But special delivery postage is very high. Can I get by with a three-cent stamp instead of a twenty-cent? Shall I fulfill this law or shall I ignore it? My action, of course, depends on how much I want the letter to be delivered in haste.

Of course we want results, but we can get them only if we follow the conditions laid down. Suppose we take a chance with traffic laws. Do we fool the laws or do we injure ourselves and others and perhaps destroy our cars? Suppose we take a chance on short measures. Do we fool our customers or do we ruin our reputation? "It is not square acres which make a country great," said Confucius, "but square men." At no time have square men been needed more desperately than today.

"Let this Mind be in you which was also in Christ Jesus." Let go and let God. Stop using the human mind and think according to Principle, and you have that *Mind.*

How did man get out of the Kingdom of God? How did he lose his place in it? By his negative thinking. How does he return to it? How can he find expression in a Kingdom of Good only? By using the Mind of Christ, by allying his thoughts with the Divinity within him. If we are praying or speaking the word for some greater good, we know that Christ is speaking the word through us. *"In all thy ways acknowledge Him, and He shall direct thy paths." "Delight thyself also in the Lord; and He shall give thee the desires of thine heart."*

The new theology has introduced a new vocabulary. The word affirmation appears often. But affirmations without conviction and substance are about as effective as swinging a prayer wheel. Jesus warned us: *"Use not vain repetitions."* Reciting a formula will accomplish nothing. *"Ye seek me because ye ate of the loaves and were filled,"* and Jesus, *"and ye cannot find me."** Putting loaves and fishes (basic necessities) before God is ignoring the Principle and ultimately ends in defeat.

Suppose, for instance, that you are making this affirmation: "The saving and protecting power of God delivers me from every adverse situation, and I am secure in Him." If you think of the personal self as making the declaration, you invoke only the power of the human mind and results will be negligible. If you think of the Christ in you as making the decree, you call upon the mighty power of God, and the results will be whatever you have in view, if those results are spiritually legal. The Father Within will do the mighty works through you.

God's Kingdom is founded on three basic facts:

1. It is a finished Kingdom.

---

* American Standard Version of the Bible.

2. It is within each of us.

3. It responds to us by corresponding to our states of mind; that is, to our consciousness.

Let us think through these statements together.

1. God's kingdom is a finished kingdom.

It is a present and spiritual state of consciousness permeating all space and time—the universe here and the everlasting now. It is a state of consciousness in which God acts through our obedience to his commandments. Jesus said to the scribe, *"Thou art not far from the Kingdom of God."* We enter this Kingdom by renewing our mind; that is, by making adjustments in our thinking and by doing the Will of God. *"Thy Kingdom come. Thy will be done."*

All the good we shall ever need is in this Kingdom now. Whatever we are seeking is seeking us. It is all on the Lord's Table, and the invitations are already out. The answer to every problem is in the fact that this Kingdom comes; that is, appears in our lives when the outer world is controlled by that which is within.

2. The Kingdom of God is within each of us.

There is something in us greater than any failure we have ever made. There is something in us greater than any disease we have ever had. There is something in us greater than any obstacle or problem we have ever met.

We have within us not only the answer to all our problems but everything necessary to make us strong, prosperous, and successful. We appropriate these spiritual blessings by releasing them through the Mind of Christ. When we change our consciousness, which is the only thing that must be changed, and think according to Principle, the whole universe begins to move into perfect action in our lives.

Working on the assumption that there are no unanswered problems and no unfulfilled desires in the universe, we start always with the premise, *"It is done."* We say with understanding and feeling. "I know that this need is fulfilled. I know that the supply I need is already established; I know that it is right for me to have it, and that in God's good time, it will appear." When you rely upon Principle, the answer may come as you have anticipated it or as a complete change in circumstances; in either case, it is God *"which worketh in you both to will and to do of his good pleasure."*

3. The Kingdom of God responds to us by corresponding to our states of mind.

The sooner we purify our minds and uproot all the erroneous ideas and troublesome beliefs the better, for they flash up into consciousness at unexpected moments and destroy our sense of spiritual values. To hold on to harmful and destructive thoughts is like trying to drive a car with water and petrol in the gas tank. The way to get rid of these undesirable thoughts and negative trends of mind is the same method by which we eliminate the foreign elements from the gas tank. We deliberately replace them with something better. When the water and other impurities have been removed, the gasoline explodes and generates power. So it is with our consciousness. When the destructive and troublesome elements have been removed, the mind of Christ, functioning under law, acts to harmonize and unify everything in our lives.

When you begin to be aware of yourself as a purely spiritual being, subject only to spiritual laws, you will be amazed at the speed and efficiency with which this concept is expressed in improved conditions in your life, in happier relationships with your fellow men, in the joy and peace within your heart.

I can ask no greater good for you as you read these pages than that the awareness of your true relationship to God and the realization of your spiritual power may come quickly, bringing to you the *"peace of God which passeth all understanding."*

Chapter II
Try Facing the Wind

One of the most thrilling things in the field of practical religion is the way in which metaphysical students meet and overcome the difficulties and misadventures of human life. Because I am a minister of Truth, many people tell me of their complicated problems and heartbreaking situations. Time and again, I am amazed at what human nature can take and awed by what it can accomplish with divine help.

The life of the average individual moves in a little orbit of its own for long periods. He establishes a way of life made up of such factors as how he thinks, the way he lives, and the manner in which he carries on the affairs of his daily life.

He has his good days and his bad days, his successes and his failures, his triumphs and his defeats; but the pattern as a whole is made up of more good than bad, more joy than grief, more pleasure than pain. His family is fairly well, his business holds its own, and his prospects are promising.

But rare is the individual for whom that rhythm is not broken dramatically at some time. As suddenly as if a ship had hit a rock in mid-ocean, tragedy strikes. Storms of many sorts sweep away all that the years have built up. A business crisis ends disastrously. Disease reaches out. "You are finished," says the doctor. "You are washed up. Put your affairs in order for you cannot live six months." Accidental death strikes down a member of the family.

But Truth students, despite adversity, go forward. Like great trees after a storm, they stand unmoved and unshaken.

I should like to retell the little story that gives the title to this chapter.*

"Hans was a shepherd boy. Every day he tended his father's sheep on the mountainside. On the last day of the old year, he led them to the south side of the mountain to get the last bit of grass before winter covered it with snow. Quite suddenly, out of the north, a storm blew up. Hans, knowing very well from experience what the hazards of a blizzard were, instantly called his dog to gather up the sheep. He, like every good shepherd, did not ordinarily drive his sheep but led them. But this day they were contrary and would not follow him against the blinding storm. Hans knew he must keep them moving into the wind; his father had always told him that if the sheep faced away from the storm, the wind would blow under their wool, drive the snow and ice next to their skin, and they would freeze. Their only hope of life was to head into the wind. So he called them, sent the dog to hip their heels, and made them face the storm. Fortunately, the direction of the storm was the way home, too. With their heads down and their eyes closed, the sheep, stumbled along, crowded against each other. Hans was out in front, the driving snow beating into his face, 'I must keep facing the wind,' he kept saying to himself, over and over. He did not know where he was or how far he had come. He ached with cold and tiredness, but the kept doggedly on, moving into the wind. Then he saw his father and his brother who had come out in search of him. When they sat down to a hot supper, his father said, 'My son, we were all frightened for you.' With tears glistening in his eyes, Hans answered, 'But I did only what you taught me, Father. I kept moving into the wind.' "

---

* Quoted by permission of J. J. Sessler.

"I keep moving into the wind," What a motto for these times! It reminds us of God's command to Moses. *"Speak unto the children of Israel that they go forward."* Going forward for them meant leaving the hardships and suffering of Egypt, but is also meant facing the peril of the Red Sea. We all know the story of the miraculous opening of the waters and the passage on dry land to the promised land of milk and honey, following their obedience to the command.

But the capacity for obedience is both Hans and the children of Israel was the result of faith.

Often we say, "If I can just make *this* demonstration; if I can just get this answer, my faith will grow by leaps and bounds." What did Jesus say to the people of His day who marveled at the power of His Word? *"All things, whatsoever ye shall ask in prayer, BELIEVING, ye shall receive."* If we have faith, if we do not doubt, if we ask believing, we shall receive what we asked for in some form. In other words, faith precedes demonstration. The signs flows. St. Paul defined faith as *"the substance of things hoped for, the evidence of things not seen."*

The disciples were terribly frightened during the storm on the Sea of Galilee. The heavens were darkened, the thunder boomed, the lightning flashed, and the winds blew. It was as though some mighty monster were trying to smash that little boat to splinters. Can you see Jesus as He walked across the deck of the boat with those terror-stricken sailors huddled about Him? Can you hear His voice as He spoke the words, *"Peace, be still?"* Can you feel the calm followed—a calm not only of the waters but of those sturdy sunburned fishermen? They had entered a new dimension—the same dimension you and I must enter if we are to meet and survive the storms of contemporary human life. William James says much the same thing in these words: "No human being every truly learns to live until he has awakened within himself the dormant powers lying there."

"I kept moving into the wind." What does the courageous indomitable person find who rides the storms of human experience? He finds what Jesus said he would find — enormous reservoirs of power to meet any need. Some writers have likened these resources of power to a second, third, and fourth wind, but it is more than that. It is another dimension of mind — that dimension of which St. Paul spoke when he said, *"I can do all things through Christ which strengtheneth me."* How did St. Paul tap these tremendous sources of power? By developing a partnership with Christ. This is not the power of wind, water, or atom, but the power of God — *"the power that worketh in you."*

We do not have to beg God for power to meet our needs. All we have to do is to relax, recognize the power, and let it flow. "But I always pray in the same way, and sometimes my prayers are not answered," you say. That may seem true to you. But sometimes you exercise real faith; and at other times, you doubt subconsciously the truth of your statements. The result is different.

Principle is unchangeable; failure in prayer is failure in application. Ralph Waldo Emerson said: "Belief is absolutely necessary: no accomplishment, no assistance, no training can compensate for lack of belief."

When you get into one of the storms we have been talking about and realize your lack of confidence, you can build faith or rebuild it at will.

Say to yourself the words of the father of the son with a dumb spirit, *"Lord, I believe; help thou mine unbelief."* Repeat the statement, *"Lord, I believe,"* and feel the truth of what you say. This won't be easy at first, for your conscious mind will deny what you say and make itself known by such thoughts as these: "This is sheer nonsense. It is for children. There is nothing to it." "You can't get through this storm. You haven't the strength. Go on and turn back."

And what will you do then? You will be more persistent and fervent than ever. You will keep saying, *"Lord, I believe,"* despite all conflict, and slowly but surely your faith will grow. Saying "I believe" is not enough. If you leave the Lord out of your belief, it falls on stony ground. This is the point on which metaphysics differs greatly from psychiatry. To be effective, belief must start with God; it must be based on a power larger than the self. The difference between power and weakness is the spiritual factor.

Why are so many people in mental hospitals today? Why are there so many psychologists and psychiatrists? Because humanity hasn't the spiritual strength to lean upon a higher power when adversity comes. When these storms arise, people tend to lose their sense of God's power to sustain them.

But most of these storms, let us note, are of our own making. They are the storms of guilt, fear, worry, jealousy, sickness, resentment hate conflict, infantile regression, and arrested development. They are the tumults in the mind and in the emotions. They are tempests in the soul. And who are the people who are most susceptible to neuroses, mental diseases, and nervous breakdowns? They are the people who live without God.

The psychiatrist has many names for these disorders; but basically, they are the outcroppings of immature and stunted souls. And the cure? We have it in the words of Isaiah: *"He will keep him in perfect peace whose mind is stayed on Thee."*

How do you meet trouble when it comes to you? Do you fold up like a deflated balloon? Do you accept it with martyred resignation? Do you, like the frightened child, give up and run away?

We are talking now about spiritual immaturity. We are talking about middle-aged people with adolescent thought-patterns, of adolescents who resort to six-year-old behavior techniques. Do you remember how St. Paul talked to the congregation in Corinth? Virtually he said, "You are old enough to eat meat, but I still have to feed you with milk. You have never grown up spiritually; you are behaving still like children." Spiritual immaturity can be a costly thing. It is not only the cause of much of our sickness, but it is also one of the chief causes of alcoholism. Somewhere in the unfoldment of the victim of alcoholism, there is an arrested development. He has never quite grown up; he has never assumed adult responsibility. Instead of facing his problems, he tries to run away. "Be your age" was one of the most forceful of slang expressions. Give the powerful possibilities in you a chance to grow along with your lengthening years.

But the bargainer still says, "Oh Lord, if you will do this for me, I will do that for you." He tries to force things out of God instead of using his faith to attract his good. He has not learned that the true prayer is the realization that God already knows his needs and is ready to fulfill them.

The successful prayer is based on faith that it is already answered. *"Before they call I will answer, and while they are yet speaking, I will hear"* is the promise.

It doesn't make any difference what your stone wall or hurdle is, God-power will enable you to get over it. No situation is impossible. Jesus says *"All things are possible"* — not a few thing but *"all things."*

Eliminate the word impossible from your vocabulary. Do you need a device to help you do this? Then take several little cards and write on them, *"With God all things are possible,"* or *"I can do all things through Christ which strengtheneth me."* Scatter these cards around so that you will see one as you shave, another as your driver your car, and still another as you work at the desk at your office. Look at them during the day and keep repeating the statement to yourself until it forms a part of you and you believe it.

Or here is another method for accomplishing the same purpose. Start on Monday morning to keep a careful record of the times you say or think that anything is impossible. Just before you go to bed, write the number down.

On Tuesday, concentrate on reducing the number of times you say or think in terms of impossibility. Write that number down Tuesday night. Keep the practice up every day until you have eliminated this form of negative thought from your consciousness.

It is true that the body and mind tend to respond to the pressure of crisis by releasing unsuspected powers. But why wait for a crisis to awaken your power? Why not release it and use it now? Why live in poverty in the midst of plenty? Why live in fear when security awaits you?

Just recently I purchased a new car which has tremendous power. When I want to pass another car quickly, I push the accelerator down to the floor, and the car fairly jumps out from under me. It is a wonderful feeling to be able to employ such power on the road, but there is an even greater power which is released through the accelerator of your mind. Start your day with an affirmation such as this: "There is but one Presence and one Power in the Universe. This Power is all good. It is in me and I am in It." Then think of the many 'manifestations of this Power. Think of the many ways in which you can use it. We boast about atomic power today, but It is weak compared to the power that Jesus ascribed to faith.

Yes, my friend, you are equal to any vicissitude or circumstance that may ever come to you. Almighty God will never permit any trouble to come into your life that you cannot face and overcome if you cooperate with Him and have faith. This is not a faith of presumption or credulity but a faith that transcends hope and fulfills expectation.

Justice Cardoza said: "We are what we believe we are." Each man has his own capacity. You can accomplish no more than you believe you can. But if you believe, you can do all things.

These words of Isaiah are comforting today: *"Be strong, fear not: behold your God will come . . . . and save you."* We know that the promise means that He will release the power of good into our affairs, that He will save us from whatever we need to be saved from.

The challenge is three-fold: buttress your faith, keep doggedly moving into the wind, and rise steadily to a higher level of maturity — to a more efficient use of your spiritual power. We do not know what a day may bring forth, but of one thing we are sure: There will be mountains to climb, bridges to build, hardships to endure, crosses to carry, and burdens to bear. How we meet these problems will be determined by our faith. If we move forward, facing each problem as it comes in faith and belief, we shall weather every storm and overcome every difficulty.

Chapter III
Try Faith in Solving Problems

In 1951, Bob Richards, the world's greatest pole vaulter, topped fifteen feet on the pole vault. He equalled the world's record in the later Olympics. When asked how he was able to attain this height, he answered, "Because of the power of the Lord." Questioned further by sports writer, he added: "Don't get the idea that some mystical power comes and lifts me over the fifteen-foot bar. It isn't that way at all. The ability is in me. And my faith in Almighty God releases that power so that I can vault a fifteen-foot bar."

When we adopt Bob's method in the approach to our difficulties, we find that we too have a power within us that is equal to our needs—a power that we can apply to any and every situation. If we keep ourselves receptive to God through our faith, His power flows through us, and we have the spiritual force necessary to surmount any obstacle or overcome any difficulty.

The great concern of Jesus about our faith was expressed in the question: *"When the Son of man cometh, shall he find faith on the earth?"* Jesus never failed to show his joy and appreciation when He found faith and He never failed to reward it. To a blind man seeking help, He said: *"Go thy way; thy faith hath made thee whole."* To another, He said, *"According to your faith, be it unto you."* To the centurion, He paid a great tribute in the words: *"I have not found so great faith, no, not in Israel."*

Faith! What a boon to those in trouble! What a joy to the sorrowing! 'What a balm to the sick! It is one of our rarest possessions—a precious jewel which we must guard night and day from everything that draws our attention away from it. When Jesus said, *"All things are possible to him that believeth,"* He was talking to you and to me and to those of all time who would carry on His transforming work.

We must have faith in God, have faith in life, have faith in ourselves, have faith in our fellowman, and have faith in His faith. *"In quietness and confidence shall be your strength"* is the promise. These words do not mean that we are to lift ourselves by our bootstraps; that is, by force of will. They mean rather that by our faith, we connect our barreness with His fullness, our weakness with His strength, our inability with His ability, our insufficiency with His sufficiency, our littleness with his greatness. We go beyond ourselves and become one with Him. We draw upon him for our needs through our faith.

In His parting message to His disciples, Jesus said, *"Ye believe in God, believe also in Me."* Again He said: *"These* [things] *have been written that ye might believe."*

Did it ever occur to you that you are what you are and have the privileges that you have because of your won or someone else's faith? The faith of your parents in one another and in you, the faith of your forefathers in the right of the individual to life, liberty, and the pursuit of happiness, the faith of your contemporaries in the need to realize adequate living conditions for very one—these are factors in your life today. Why is it that the banker will cash a check for one man and not for another? Why do we so happily accept folding money? Back of acceptance of any symbol, there must be faith, confidence, and belief. The whole structure of our living rest upon faith. If faith fails, everything else falls with it.

But faith, let us note, is not so much holding on to God, as it is letting God hold on to us. The man who goes places and accomplishes things does not know in advance just where he will arrive. Traveling by faith, he has no chart, evidence, or experience to go by. He is prepared to accept anything that happens and to find it good. He is aware that his life follows a plan which he cannot see — a plan that results from the action of the All-Seeing, All-Knowing, All-Powerful Father.

The words of Jesus lift the individual out of the mass and clothe · him with uniqueness, with significance, with importance, with confidence: *"Are not five sparrows sold for two farthings, and not one of them is forgotten before God? But even the very hairs of your · head are all numbered. Fear not therefore: ye are of more value than many sparrows."*

"Behold the fowls of the air: for they sow not, neither do they reap, nor gather into barns; yet your heavenly Father feedeth them. Are ye not much better than they?"

"Consider the lilies of the field, how they grow; they toil not neither do they spin. . . . Wherefore if God so clothe the grass of the field, shall he not much more clothe you?"

Where did you get the idea that you needed a lot of faith to overcome the difficulties and adversities in your life? Is faith a matter of quantity or of quality? The question you have to answer is not "How much faith do I have?" but "How real is my faith? Is it free from doubt? Is is steadfast? Does it stand up in a crisis?"

Deep in every man's heart is the belief in a Power greater than himself. He may be many years and countless miles away from the time and place in which he last overtly recognized that Power, but the belief is only dormant; it is not dead.

St. Paul said to Timothy, *"Stir up the gift of God which is in thee,"* referring to what he called *"the unfeigned faith."*

Jesus said, *"If ye have faith as a grain of mustard seed, ye shall say to this mountain, Remove hence to yonder place; and it shall remove; and nothing shall be impossible unto you."*

Do you find fault with your experiences in life? Then get a set of beliefs that will result in different attitudes. Abraham Lincoln said, "Accept all you can by reason and the rest by faith, and you will live and die a better man."

There is no hope for the man who persistently says "It can't be done." He has shut himself off from God. St. Mark says of Jesus' work in one area, *"He could do no mighty works there because of their unbelief."* Actually, the worst thing that can happen to any man is his acceptance of loss o f faith. A faithless man is literally a lost man.

Why is it that one person is strengthened by his problem while another is weakend by it? The same catastrophe happens to two persons; one goes down while the other goes up. The difference is the result of their different attitudes. Like an insect trying to climb out of a slippery bowl, one tries to meet his problem from the surface of his ·mind with personal power. The other man lets God solve the problem for him.

There are two famous pictures of Daniel in the lions' den. In one Daniel stands facing the lions trying to overcome them by his own strength. In the other, Daniel is not thinking of the lions at all; he stands with his back toward them, facing God, who is represented by a shaft of light. The first picture illustrates a commonplace error in metaphysical practice. If, facing a problem, you rely on your own strength and wisdom, you will fail. If, however, you look away from the difficulty and look steadfastly to God, your need is met.

Remember that a problem has no reality or substance apart from your mind. It is only when you recognize a circumstance or condition as a problem that it becomes real. That is why it is wise to postpone handling a problem until it is at least twenty-four hours old. You must have a chance to relax tension and develop a perspective in order to think straight about it.

In reality, the only problem in any problem is to give more of your faith to God and less of it to the condition which is troubling you. God comes into the situation when you let the *"Mind be in you which was also in Christ Jesus."*

Never identify yourself with a difficulty; *"Cast your burdens upon the Lord."* Say, *"I live; yet not I, but Christ liveth in me.* [It is no longer my problem but God's.]" Your part is to keep God in the forefront of consciousness, and He in turn will govern all your affairs. Practice His Presence. Think about Him as many times each day as you can. Walk with Him, talk with Him, put your problems lovingly in His Hands, and believe that He is helping you.

Say something like this to the problem that seems to face you: " *'Be thou removed* [that is, get out of my life], *and be thou cast into the sea.'* You have no place in my life. There is nothing in my consciousness for a problem to work with. I see through this trouble to the Divine Presence within me. I know that this problem is already solved by Divine Love. I believe that it will speedily cease to be a part of my outward experience.

"There is nothing in my consciousness that can doubt, deny, or delay the perfect outcome of this prayer. There is nothing that can weaken or dissipate the clear realization of my faith. I speak this word with absolute confidence, faith, and acceptance. I know that my word *'shall not return unto me void, but shall accomplish that which I please, and it shall prosper in the thing where to I sent it.'* I know that it will put to an end all these things that are troubling me. I accept the fulfillment of this desire now."

Then center your thought on the fulfilled wish. Get the realization that the work is done; assume thee feeling of competition. Know that all the claims you have made will be carried out as you have believed.

"But this is a very large claim," you say. That may be true to sense, but I speak to you of a dimension in which faith gets very large results—not a watered-down faith that ends in a feeble hope that something can or may happen to change things but a faith that actually becomes the wish fulfilled.

Do you remember that Jesus said to the woman with the issue of blood, *"Thy faith hath made thee whole"*? Not *my* faith, but *thy* faith. The same faith is lying quiescent in you now—the faith in a Power that opens blind eyes, unstops deaf ears, heals broken bodies, restores broken friendships, breaks down barriers, removes difficulties, prospers the poor, and strengthens the weak. There is a glorious revelation in this statement, and I want you to see it. The word thy not only places the responsibility for healing upon an individual's faith but shows that the entire operation takes place within his consciousness. Skill in praying demands not only that we have faith but also that we have acceptance and agreement. If there is no doubt in the heart (the subconscious mind) of the one who prays, *"those things which he saith shall come to pass; he shall have whatsoever he saith."*

Here then are four simple rules for meeting your problems:

1. Realize that your cooperation with God is much more important than the solution to your problem.

2. Instead of asking God to solve your problem, ask Him for wisdom to comply with the divine plan under which all problems are solved.

3. Withdraw the thought-substance from your problem by refusing to give it power.

4. Keep your thinking and your faith together.

Would you really like to prove God? Would you really like to release the greatest power in the world? Then *"stir up the gift of God* [faith], *which is within thee."* I repeat that command because it is the basis of all meta · physical practice. Know with St. John that *"This is the victory that overcometh the world, even our faith."*

Chapter IV
Try Faith in a Plan

The title does not imply that one must outline step by step what he hopes to achieve what he desires to accomplish, for this type of planning disregards the fact that a Divine Intelligence is active in our affairs. Too often this kind of planner cannot make the adjustment to an unexpected turn or development and is thrown into a state of paralysis, or inactivity by it. He has virtually said, "God, this is the way I want you to do this." He wants God to go along with him, not realizing that he should go along with God. He cannot realize that the new turn of events may in the long run be far better than the one he has outlines.

But there is a kind of planning that is imperative. Even Jesus planned. If you recall before the feeding of the five thousand on the shore of Galilee, He asked Philip, *"Whence shall we buy bread that these may eat?"* and the next verse tells us that *"He himself knew what he would do."*

In the twelfth chapter of the Epistle o the Hebrews, you will find a plan based on the right kind of activity — a plan which can transmute your mental picture into a reality. St. Paul says, *"Wherefore, seeing we are compassed about with a great cloud of witnesses, let us lay aside every weight, and the sin which doth so easily beset us, and let us run with patience the race that is set before us, looking unto Jesus the author · and finisher of our faith."*

There are four phases of St. Paul's directions:

The first — *"compassed about with a great cloud of witnesses"* — implies that we must consider the lives of those around us, particularly those who accept the responsibility of living by the Spiritual Law. St. Paul was, of course, speaking of and to persons who were known to be followers of Jesus, those we refer to now as the first Christians.

The second demand is that we *"Lay aside every weight."*

The third challenges us to *"Run with patience the race that is set before us,"* and the fourth to *"Look to Jesus, the author and finisher of our faith."*

Let us think through these four parts in turn. St. Paul was talking to people who were having a difficult time. He was trying to encourage them by telling them of others who had the same difficulties and overcame them; of those who were successful in the end. This was good psychology; it strengthened the faith of those who were still striving for mastery. Today, we need this same type of encouragement. We need to see that some part of our time is spent in the company of those who are attempting to live by Principle. We need to set aside a period of the day for reading articles and books that are helpful to our thinking and meditating. These activities should be an integral part of our plan.

We must awake to the Truth that the potentially of one is the potentiality of all and know that what one person can do, another can do. We see around us those who have faced difficulty, sorrow, and tribulation and have triumphed over these conditions. Of course, we see others who have been defeated.

What is it that makes the difference between success and failure? First of all, it is necessary to get the picture of success clearly and firmly fixed in your mind. Make an obsession of it. Keep it steadily in the forefront of consciousness to succeed and that there is nothing in the universe that can interfere.

Failure and success like gloom and happiness are habits. Some people develop such a consciousness of failure that there is no room in them for success.

But the failure does not need to stay the way he is. Lord Halifax said, "If you hold a thought long enough, that thought will take you prisoner." That is a law of mind. A prisoner of thought, however, is a voluntary prisoner who can secure his release by changing his thinking.

When we think of the *"cloud of witnesses"* that compass us about today, we must be aware of the great body of evidence that exists as to the effect on the life of struggling humanity of its acceptance of oneness with God — of man's realization of his divinity — of his recognition of the Father Within — of his awareness of the Indwelling God.

Then *"Lay aside every weight,"* says St. Paul. That is get rid of all the impediments you carry. Get rid of all this excess baggage that is weighing you down. Cast out your animosity, fear, worry, temper, and jealousy. Stop looking for trouble, for symptoms, for the worst. Forget the woes of the past. Develop a good forgettery.

Memory is a wonderful faculty of the mind. To be able to retain information and recall events is often of great importance. Of greater importance to one's personal life, however, is the ability to drop from the mind bitterness, grief, unhappiness, and resentments; to be able to say, "I will hold this good in my memory, but that evil I shall cast from me." If you wish to be happy and successful, you must cultivate the art of forgetting. You must learn to be selective in what you remember.

Many of our troubles are due to the memory of old hurts, old guilts, old fears, old resentments, old dislikes, old grudges, and old negative experiences. Sometimes we feed on these most deliberately — regurgitating them, as it were. Other adverse memories we push back become a part of our subconscious minds. Understanding of one's self and faith in a Power greater than we are, are essential to proper handling of disagreeable memories, which can truly become the "weights" of which St. Paul spoke.

Norman Vincent Peale's comments[*] on an address by Dr. John Albert Schindler of Wisconsin are pertinent. He says, "Dr. Schindler makes the point that in this country fifty from psychosomatic causes. That is they are ill not because they succumbed to a germ or developed an organic disease or were victims of accidents but because they allowed their thoughts and emotions to be set into wrong patterns. He quotes from the records of a clinic in New Orleans from a study that was made five hundred consecutive patients. Three of five hundred and eighty, or seventy-six percent, were, afflicted by psychosomatic causes. They were filled with fear; they had a sense of guilt. If they had all gone to church, read the Bible prayed, had faith in God and obeyed Him, attended to their own business and behaved themselves, they would not have been ill. That is about the size of it.

"This doctor, who must be a whimsical, salty. Will Rogers kind of character, insists that psychosomatic is not an adequate name for this kind of disease. He calls it C.D.T.'s for it is an accumulation of Cares, Difficulties, and Troubles that take over the mind and gradually, like a cloud, obscure the sun and leave one walking in a gathering mental darkness. Unless occasionally one breaks through this heavy covering of care, difficulties, troubles, and get the mind into an area of joy, gradually he becomes a psychosomatic problem."

---

[*] Quoted by permission of Norman Vincent Peale.

These are the *"weights"* which St. Paul was talking about and to recall them without destroying their power is most detrimental to the thinker. It doesn't thinker. It doesn't make any difference whether a thought is old or new, the minute that you resurrect it, the instant that you put your attention upon it, it becomes active. The only sensible practice is to concentrate upon desirable experiences and memories. No matter what the past has held, we can at any moment start all over again.

St. Paul then tells us to *"run with patience."* The *"patience"* referred to is not endurance but perseverance and steadfastness. Man was not meant to beat out his life with pressure, friction, rancor, and burning discontent. He was given this world to live successfully and happily in. Patience is not a sign of weakness but of strength. Waiting is not a sign of dawdling and drifting but of alertness and expectancy. Wait; do not dig up and destroy your dream. Give it a chance to germinate and to grow. *"Set yourselves, stand ye still, and see the salvation of the Lord with you,"* said the Lord to the children of Judah.

Did you ever count the failures that are due to impatience — the unfinished tasks and the unanswered prayers? Their number is legion. *"Couldst not thou watch one hour?"* asked Jesus of Simon Peter.

Before God calls men to great tasks. He tests their patience. Moses sent into the wilderness to Horeb to tend sheep; Elijah into the dried-up river bed of Kedron. Paul lived in the desert of Arabia, and Jesus spent forty lonely years in the wilderness of Judea.

Not many of us realize how much our health and supply hinge upon patience. We are not naturally patient. When we want a thing, we want it now. We often desire it so intensely that if we cannot have it immediately, we lose all interest in it. The word *patience* is used many times in the Bible and there are many marginal references to the word *steadfastness.* *Resignation* is sometimes given as a synonym for patience, but in our thinking they have a different application. If there is no way out of a given situation, *resignation* is the word.

I think this point is well illustrated by the little boy whose Aunt had died. A very religious man under the old thought, met the little nephew on the street, and after expressing his sympathy asked the common question: "was your Aunt resigned?" The boy looked up at the man in amazement, and with childlike abruptness and simplicity burst out: "Resigned? Shucks, she had to be."

Actually this is what resignation amounts to. IF you have to, you have to. If there is no way out of a situation you must put up with it. You must accept it and make the best of it. But the true idea of patience is that of steadfastness and perseverance.

Jesus spent thirty years in training for a ministry. of three years, but think of he power and far reaching effect of that ministry. Compare it, for instance, with the training of metaphysical students who expect to arrive at spiritual maturity in six, eight, or ten weeks. It is any wonder that so many stumble and fall by the wayside? They forget that it takes years to build a consciousness of Truth. They are lacking in steadfastness and perseverance. *"In your patience,"* said Jesus, *"possess ye your souls."*

Most of us think of patience as a period in which we sit down, fold our hands, and do nothing. St. Paul says, *"Run with patience."* Get going and keep yourself in action, but remain calm. Stop trying to make things happen. Keep your light burning in the darkness. Do one thing at a time but keep at it. Remember the jingle:

"All things come to him who waits,
But here's a rule that's slicker:
The man who goes for what he wants,
Will get it all the quicker."

"Looking unto Jesus" is Paul's third condition. The implication is clear. Stop depending upon will power. Stop looking to others. Have an undivided mind. Look to God the source of all Good. To look to Him in faith is to receive what you ask for. Leave self out of the picture altogether. *"Of mine own self, I can do nothing." "The father that dwelleth in me, He doeth the works,"* said Jesus of his miracles on earth.

Think of the things people do when they forget self. Under the stimulus of some great emotion, man discovers strength and abilities that he did not know he had. In a fire, for instance, a fourteen-year-old girl drags a two-hundred-pound man out of doors to safety. An eight-year-old friend seeing a five-hundred-pound barn door fall upon a little boy rushed forth and lifted it up by herself. She lifted what two or three men ordinarily could not have lifted. When you take your attention away from the problem and draw upon your inner strength, the problem disintegrates and falls away. *"Looking unto Jesus"* means that you must stop trying to think your way out of your difficulties; there is an easier and a much more permanent way of removing them.

Until man realizes that God is greater than the instrument through which He expresses, he misuses and subverts the power that alone can make him whole. Peter thought that he could walk on the water with Jesus and started bravely; but seeing the wind, he thought of himself and of what he was doing and began to sink. If my little old lady friend who lifted the heavy door had thought of what she was doing, she could not have done it. She thought of the child's need. There is an explanation of her sudden access to power. Do you remember the words of Jesus as he took a child in his arms at Capernaum, *"Whosoever shall receive one of such children. . . . receiveth me"?* And that all-inclusive statement that forces us not only to recognize our unity with God but our unity with our fellow-man — *"Inasmuch as ye have done it unto the least of these my brethren, ye have done it unto me"?*

Before you can do that which cannot be done, you must not only be *"absent from the body* [self]*"* but *"present with the Lord,"* according to St. Paul.

"Looking unto Jesus" means not only lifting up your mind to God, but surrendering all sense of personal responsibility, all notions about hurry, pressure, stewing, straining, fretting, and taxing of human strength. We must be absent from personality. We must forego fears, worries, disappointments, perplexities, jealousies, frustrations, and despair. We must burn our martyr's crown.

Is your body sick and weak? Then turn away from this outer appearance and look to God. Lift up your heart so that you may receive help directly from God. Claim His peace, His harmony, and His wholeness. Dare to sense His Omnipotence as you make your claim for health.

Have you a task to perform that causes you to doubt your ability? Are you jittery fearful, undecided, worried, and puzzled? Then look unto Jesus, and place yourself and your problem lovingly in His hands. Be patient. The answer will come. Turn your attention from self and look to God, and marvelous changes will take place.

St. Paul has given us a wonderful four-step plan:

1. Be receptive to spiritual help.

2. Live understandingly in the present.

3. Wait upon the Lord.

4. Recognize your unity with God.

If we carry this plan out, if we pattern our lives on it with faith in our power to use the divine help that we know is available, we shall truly know that *"peace of God"* which we seek.

Chapter V
Try Faith in Action

Over the stage of the Goodman Theatre in Chicago are the words, "You, yourselves, must set the flame to the fagots you have brought." That might well serve as a motto for every Truth student in the land. The trouble with most of us is that we do not practice what we know. Do you remember the story of the mother who said she was glad she had two sons, one a minister and the other a doctor, so that one could preach and the other practice?

St. James said, *"Be ye doers of the word, and not hearers only, deceiving your own selves."* Perhaps we have been substituting knowing for feeling, hearing for doing. Under the barrage of verbal metaphysics, we tend to be mostly ears. We are like the pious Buddhist that J. Wallace Hamilton tells about.

"The Buddhist died and went to heaven and was taken on a tour of his new home. Kwannon, the goddess of mercy who was his guide, showed his treasures. There was a brilliant mansion which held gold and precious stones to dazzle his eyes with their luster another mansion from which angel songs filled the air, a lovely garden of lotus flowers. It was all beautifully and satisfying, for it was exactly as he had pictured heaven, until they to a room that looked like a merchant's shop. Lining the wall were shelves on which were piled and labeled what might have dried mushrooms. On closer examination, the Buddhist saw that they were actually human ears. 'You see,' explained the goddess, 'these are the ears of the people who, on earth went diligently to service, listened with pleasure to the teachings of the gods, and did nothing about what they heard. After death *they* went elsewhere but their ears were saved. Only their faithful ears reached heaven."

This story fits in with St. Paul's declaration that *"Faith without works is dead."*

Outlining an objective for action is life is all too easy for most of us, but without the persistent action of faith and practice to back it up, it remains in the mental sphere and nothing come of it. I like the story Richard Lynch tell of a man who built himself a cottage on the shore of a lake. Some one liked it and wanted to buy it. The builder sold it and built himself another. The same thing happened again. He built another and another, and the demand for his cottages increased until quite a group had been built and sold. Some one suggested that a hotel was needed to complete the colony. One day the original builder was seen at work out in a cleared space. When the curious people asked what he was doing, he answered that he was erecting a chimney for the hotel that he would build around it when he got the money. Needless to say, the hotel was built. By his action he sat flame to the fagots of his plan. Working out a vision, staking your life on the outcome of your faith, blazing a trail, disregarding appearances, doing the impossible, being true to something beyond yourself— these are the evidences of faith.

The basic factor in the successful application of Divine Law is not the number of books you read, the number of classes you take, nor the number of lecture you hear; it is your faith. William James, the great psychologist, said, "In any project, the one important factor is your belief. Without belief there can be no demonstration." That statement is basic. The idea (the mental equivalent of that which you desire) exists first in the mind. Then the acceptance of the idea by the consciousness gives it power to clothe itself in form through your faith.

God gave man mastery and domination, but man has lost his perspective and reversed his power. Believing that the world is the positive factor and he the negative, he has subjected himself to circumstances and conditions to the opinions and the judgments of humanity. Only as he practices faith in Good does he find that he is the positive being and that the world is increasingly subject to his word. Only then does he prove that faith in God overcomes every difficulty.

Faith is not a function of any particular mental faculty; it is, rather, the action of the entire consciousness. It is desiring and knowing that your word will be heard, that it will be acted upon, and that it will take form. It is your conviction that you have the power to make a demand on the universe that will be honored. To believe is to have. St. Paul said, *"Faith is the substance of things hoped for, the evidence of things not seen."* Faith is the hope and the result, the vision and the form, seedtime and harvest, prayer and answer, wish and fulfillment. Synchronizing thought, imagination, desire, feeling, and will with faith produces action.

The Law of Faith is at all ties working for or against you. Would you then deliberately chose to have faith in evil, in weakness, in sickness, and in poverty, when by the same deliberate choice you can have faith in good, in strength, in health, in plenty? It is as true that performance generates faith as that idleness generates doubt.

Why, then, do you sit around bemoaning your fate, looking only toward the obvious and complaining about conditions and lack of opportunities? Yes, I know, you have probably attempted to meet your problems with push-button prayers, but now is the time to try something else. For hopes and wishes, substitute faith and works; Just as the muscles of your body require exercise, your faith must be quickened within you. It must be developed through practice so that it will register in accomplishment. It must be. turned from a possibility into a potentiality. It must be raised from a fire cracker to an atomic bomb.

"To increase our faith," says Craig Carter, "we should treat ourselves to know that Truth even now is expressing in, through, and for us and that we can count upon it." If we say this sentence aloud as a fact in which we believe, we have given ourselves a treatment for faith. That is the way it works. It is that simple.

The simplest form of metaphysical treatment is to say aloud in our own words the Divine Truth, as best we understand it about the condition being treated. Such a statement constitutes a demand upon Law for the demonstration of the Truth stated.

There are many ways of cultivating faith but the simplest the way is to affirm it—to declare that you have it. The shortest affirmation to accomplish this is probably this statement: "I have faith in God—Good. My faith overcomes every difficulty."

Hold this statement in your mind until it forms in you · a consciousness of itself. "But I have no faith," you say. That doesn't make any difference. Act as though you had it. As Shakespeare said: "Assume a virtue if you have it not." Affirm faith and keep affirming it until you feel it. Give out faith to others, and faith will come back to you. Faith is contagious; get close to those who have it. · Seize every opportunity to exercise your faith. Keep telling yourself that you have faith and remember that all action takes place within you.

Are you determined to get rid of all the inferior, weak, negative, and defeatist thoughts in your subconscious mind, and to build a sustaining consciousness of the Presence of God? Then begin to act at this moment.

We don't get more faith by merely wishing we had more; we get it but by expressing what we have in daily actions.

Someone has said that "faith in action is the concentration of all one's mental and spiritual powers upon the reality of God's perfection to such a degree that all other thoughts are blotted out of mind. They no longer exist." When you exercise your faith in God, you are knowing nothing but the Presence and Power of God in every condition, difficulty, circumstance, and situation. You are making your belief so strong, so all-important, so all-absorbing, so all-inclusive that the mental substance in your difficulty is dissolved and the problem for the moment drops out of your thoughts. If you have been in the habits of thinking negatively about circumstances, conditions, persons, and things, start now to think in terms of faith.

It isn't going to be easy at first if you have been accepting defeat and frustration for so long that it has become a habit, if you have come to feel that you have no faith left. But the old mistakes have nothing to do with the new program of action. Your faith is there waiting to be put to work.

Don't go around telling people that you wish you had a so-and-so's faith. You do not want anybody's else's faith. You want your own. God made you to fill important places, to do big things. It doesn't make any difference how far down the ladder at the moment you may be nor how hopeless your situation seems. If you will put your faith to work, you can climb to the top with the words: "My faith overcomes every difficulty."

In reality, there is no formula for faith; but there are techniques which we can make our own. Remember four things as you put your desire to increase your faith to work.

1. There is a Universal Law that operates upon faith.

2. Like the laws of electricity and gravity, It is not only always present but It is also instantly responsive to your call.

3. It does for you only what It can do *through* you.

4. Its action is always commensurate with the degree of your belief.

When Jesus touched the eyes of the two blind men and healed them, He said, "According to your faith, be it done unto you." He not only announced the nature of faith but described the way in which it works. On another occasion, He said, *"As thou hast believed, so be it done unto thee."* What did He mean? He was saying that there is a mighty, propelling Law in the universe that operates with and through and upon your faith and that it is immediate and invincible.

Consider the words, *"as thou hast believed."* The action of the Law is always limited by your belief. If you hold up a large measure to the universe, you have a large return. If you hold up a small measure, you have a meager return. The size of the measure (the mental equivalent) is always determined by you. *"Prove me now herewith, saith the Lord of Hosts, if I will not open you the windows of heaven and pour you out a blessing, and there shall not be room enough to receive it."*

Have you a tough problem to solve or a seemingly impassable barrier to cross? Then bring to bear upon it the power of an indomitable, invincible faith in the Law of Good. Instead of thinking negatively about the problem, think in the positive terms of accomplishment, of victory, of completion, of success. Keep your trolley on the wire. Keep God in the forefront of consciousness and the Creative Force flowing through you, and the problem will be solved, the barrier crossed or eliminated.

Have you come to the end of your rope? Then tie a knot in it and hang on. Right where you are at this moment is the answer to your smallest or your greatest need, the fulfillment of your every desire. Dare to act on the magic of these words: "My faith in God overcomes every difficulty." Roll them around in your mind. Say them over and over. Say them out loud. Say them until they set up a suction in your mind. Say them until your whole consciousness accepts them, and they become a living, vitalizing power in your life.

"MY FAITH IN GOD OVERCOMES EVERY DIFFICULTY."

These seven words are literally packed with vital, dynamic, creative power. Think about them, meditate upon them, dwell with them until they sink into your subconscious mind. Act upon them consciously until they become automatic in your life. Know with all your heart, mind, strength, and soul that the Truth they carry has the power to transform your world — the authority to banish every difficulty — the capacity to meet every need.

Chapter VI
Try Faith in Healing

1.

"RISE UP AND WALK!"

The words are a command. Something wonderful follows it.

"Look at the beggar over there by the gate of the temple. That old human wreck has been there since I was a child—over fifty years, I've heard my father say."

"Something seems to be happening to him. See, a man is taking him by the hand and lifting him up. What on earth is going on?"

"Let's hurry over and see. My word, he is walking! And leaping!"

"He is shouting and praising God. He is really walking toward the temple under his own power."

"Can it be possible that that helpless bundle of flesh and bones has been healed?"

"Wonder of wonders, he surely has!"

"Think of the state of his body after all the years of dirt and filth. Think of the years his muscles have not been used. In spite of it all, he is back on his feet and walking by himself."

"Amazing! I wouldn't have believed it if I hadn't seen it myself."

2.

"EPHPHATHA, THAT IS, BE OPENED."

Here is another command and another scene.

"Poor foolish dumb man! How can he expect to be cured? He's been that way all his life."

"How can he expect to hear and speak now? Why doesn't he forget the whole thing and make the best of it?"

"That's what I say? Why do they kid him? Why build up his hopes?"

"It is presumptuous of him to expect healing."

Can you visualize the scene? Watch the Master as *"He took him aside from the multitude, and put his fingers in his ears, and . . . touched his tongue, . . . and saith unto him, Ephphatha, that is, Be opened. And straightway his ears were opened, and the string of his tongue was loosed, and he spoke plain."*

3.

"BE OF GOOD COMFORT: THY FAITH HATH MADE THEE WHOLE."

Again a command, but this time a recognition in words of the part the faith of the woman played in the healing.

"If I may but touch His garment, I shall be whole," she said to herself.

But can't you hear what others were saying?

"Imagine a woman ill for twelve years seeking to be healed. She's pinning her faith on one thing and that so simple! "

"She's certainly getting ready for a big letdown."

"Have you ever known such tenacity? She's been to all the doctors and spent all her money looking for a cure. Now she's turning to Christ and expects to be healed."

"What audacity!"

She is audacious. Faith is always audacious, bold, unquestioning. Hers may be a little thin after twelve years, but she is ready to try again. Jesus was passing on his way to the house of Jesus. As the crowd moved along with Him it was easy for her to come close enough to touch the hem of His garment, and her healing occurred at that moment.

But now the unexpected · happens. Jesus turns and demands, *"Who touched me?"*

"Master, the multitude throng thee and press thee."

"Somebody hath touched me: for I perceive virtue hath gone out of me."

Then came her halting explanation, and the reassurance from Jesus, *"Be of good comfort* [Don't be afraid. You did just the right thing.]; *thy faith hath made thee whole."*

4.

"BE IT UNTO THEE EVEN AS THOU WILT."

Again a command, but note the determining factor in what happens.

"Have mercy on me, O Lord, thou Son of David; my daughter is grievously vexed with a devil," a woman of Canaan cries.

"Send her away," say the disciples, *"for she crieth after us."*

This woman is a Gentile, and Jesus says, *"I am not sent but unto the lost sheep of the house of Israel."*

That rebuff would have been enough for most people, but she responds quickly with another plea, *"Lord, help me."*

Again Jesus seizes the opportunity — talking this time, no doubt, for the disciples, too. *"It is not meet to take the children's bread and cast it to dogs."*

That was pretty rough treatment and not at all like Jesus, but he was making a point. Dogs was a term which the Jews used to express their antagonism and contempt for the Gentiles. This was another rebuff, but again the woman was quick on the trigger.

"Truth, Lord: yet the dogs eat the crumbs which fall from their master's table."

Her argument was so convincing that it overcame every other consideration. Jesus exclaimed *"Oh woman, great is thy faith: be it unto thee even as thou wilt."*

St. Matthew closes his report by saying, *"And her daughter was made whole from that very hour."*

5.

"STRETCH FORTH THINE HAND."

This was the command to the man with a withered hand . . . a test case if there ever was one, for the Pharisees were quibbling with Him as to His actions on the Sabbath day.

How many times had the victim heard such words as these, do you suppose?

"My! My! What a terrible looking hand!"

"How did it ever get that way? Did you have an accident?"

"Is it a bum?"

What did Jesus do and see as the arm was stretched forth at His command? Did he delve into the man's past history? Did he see the degeneration of the muscles, the shriveled skin, the shrunken hand? No, looking with the upper eye, He saw a perfect hand. There was nothing to be changed, corrected, or removed. He looked through the unreality of the man's belief and saw the perfection of Reality.

"Then saith he to the man, Stretch forth thine hand. And he stretched it forth; and it was restored whole, like as the other."

6.

Jesus was leaving Jericho with His disciples when a blind man sitting by the roadside cried out, *"Jesus, thou Son of David, have mercy on me."* The disciples, fearing that Jesus might be overworking and overtaxing His strength, tried to shut the man up. "Hold your peace," they shouted. *"But he cried the more a great deal, Thou Son of David, have mercy on me."* There was nothing else to do. Jesus stood still and commanded him to be called. *"And they called the blind man, saying unto him, Be of good comfort, rise; he calleth thee. And he, casting away his garment, rose, and came to Jesus. And Jesus answered and said unto him, What wilt thou that that I should do unto thee?"*

Jesus knew what the blind man wanted, and the blind man knew what he wanted. Without a moment's hesitation, he answered, *"Lord, that I might receive my sight.* [I want to see. I must see.]*"* Now listen to Jesus' response to that wholehearted appeal: *"Go thy way; thy faith hath made thee whole. And immediately he received his sight and followed Jesus in the way."*

7.

"And Jesus seeing their faith said unto the sick of the palsy; Son, be of good cheer; thy sins be forgiven thee . . . Arise, take up thy bed, go unto thine house." Here the inference is plain; forgiveness precedes healing. The state of the soul determines the health of the body. When Jesus gave His followers the commission to heal the sick, He also gave them the authority to forgive sin, for if there is a maladjustment in the soul, there will be a maladjustment in the body. Healing comes through a realignment with the Perfect Mind and Law of God.

"If thou return to the Almighty thou shalt be built up."

"But that is all ancient history," you say.

That is true, but what has changed in the long periods of time? Is the human body still not subject to disease? Do we not still seek help from the physician? And aren't there countless persons (you among them) who realize that healing is a definite responsibility of religion?

The only thing that has changed is that Jesus no longer walks the earth in human form. But Christ is still the certificated channel through which the healing power of God is poured forth. He is still the manifestation in consciousness of the accessibility, helpfulness, and power of God. He is still the medium through which God and man meet.

"But," you say, "how can this be since Jesus took His body out of the here into the everywhere?"

That is just the point. That is the answer to your question. In the everywhere, He is instantly available to all men. Christ is not a person, as we are persons. He is the Principle of Life which indwells all men. He is the Living Spirit always present with us. He is the Savior, the Divine Healer. By Savior, we mean the Saving Presence; to touch this Presence is to shift all human burdens and difficulties from our shoulders to His. Since He is Omnipresent and Omnipotent, we can place all reliance upon Him. If we accept Him, if we have faith, He goes before us and makes easy, successful, and safe our way. He takes over the government of our lives — healing, renewing, revitalizing, restoring, readjusting, and rebuilding us.

The words, *"Christ in you,"* do not mean that He is located somewhere in our bodies; He is in our consciousness — "nearer is He than breathing and closer than hands and feet." He is right where we are at every moment of every day, occupying the same space that we occupy, awaiting our recognition. Being Omnipresent He is always with us in His fullness.

Wherever we are, all of God is. Are these just words to you? Perhaps you are tired of psychological mumbo jumbo and mental gymnastics. Then follow His advice, *"Become as a little child."* Open your consciousness to His Presence. When you succeed, you will do away with all formality and all the complex thought processes. You will just sit in the Presence and wait for It to fill all the vacant places in your life.

If you read the seven selections from the New Testament thoughtfully, you recognized three conditions which those seeking healing must meet:

1. The desire or intent must be clear. *("What will ye that I should do?")*

2. Faith must be present. *("Believest thou this?")*

3. Forgiveness must be given and received.

Are you seeking healing? Then remember that it is the same search—the same Presence—the same Law—the same healing—the same *"Christ in you the hope of glory"* that you have been reading about.

He is asking you now, *"What wilt thou?* [What do you want? Do you know what you want? Are you willing to take the responsibility that will follow the materialization of your desire? Is it spiritually legal; that is, will it harm no one?] "

This is your big moment—your great opportunity. This is the day you have been waiting for. This is the day when something wonderful is going to happen to you. You have sought help from many sources, and now you are face to face with the Great Physician. You are in the Presence of the Christ who not only can but will heal you of whatever is troubling you. *"If thine eye be single* [if you see your want in its entirety], *thy whole body shall be full of light."* Can you meet the firs t test? Do you know what you want? Have you made up your mind? Is your picture clear?

Perhaps you are saying, "I want to be healed," "I want the answer to this prayer," "I want greater income," "I want the solution to this business problem," "I want to be reconciled to my friend," "I want forgiveness of my sins," "I want greater spiritual understanding. "

And all the while, the Christ stands here by your side saying, *"What wilt thou that I should do unto thee?"* This is an invitation. Tell Him what is on your mind. *"Lord, that I might receive my sight.* [Lord, that this cataract may be removed.]" "Lord, that I may walk." "Lord, that I may be freed from this false appetite from this sense of guilt." "Lord, that I may grow in spiritual understanding."

Now move on to the next step. *"Believe ye that I am able to do this?"* Let's have a little self-examination. Are you going to say, *"Lord, I believe; help thou mine unbelief"*? Just imagine that the Christ is right there in the room with you. You do have faith, but perhaps it isn't fully established. Maybe there is still a little doubt in it — a little denial. But you want this demonstration. It is the most pressing and urgent need in your life — *"Help thou mine unbelief.* [Help my frailty. Help my ignorance. Increase my consciousness. Give me understanding. Supply my lack.]"

He is asking you now, "Does your faith work for or against you?" "Does it move forward or backward?" "Do you believe that this healing is possible?" "Do you believe this need can be met?" *"Believest thou this?"* He asks. How large is your acceptance? How spacious are your capacities? How comprehensive is your faith? How much can you believe?

He doesn't ask where or what you have studied, nor how many doctors or practitioners you've had. He is interested only in your faith. He is inquiring, "Just what do you believe about yourself? About Me? How far are you willing to go with Me? How much persistency do you have? Has your study of metaphysics given you a consciousness of Truth? Are you able to accept what you ask for? Can you say, *'Yea, yea, Lord,'* and mean It?"

No wavering now. No side-stepping. Either you believe or you don't. Don't think one thing and say another. The Christ is here and this demonstration depends upon you—upon your consciousness, your faith, and your acceptance. Now, tell me. Have you heard of anyone who has had a remarkable answer to prayer? Do you know of anyone who has ever demonstrated supply through consciousness? Do you know of anyone anywhere who has ever been healed by spiritual means without the medium of surgery or medicine? There is your faith, and that is all the faith you will ever need. "God is no respecter of persons." What one has done, all can do. The potentiality of one is the potentiality of all.

Take this faith and use it. Put it to work now. *"Lord, I believe."* God is to you exactly what you conceive Him to be. Do you see the logic of all this? When you are convinced that God is, that God can, that God will, you have found your Source of Power. God, however is not to be brought down to the size of your faith; you must be lifted up to His faith.

1.

"What kind of God do you have?" I ask a patient.

"Well, I am not sure. There are times that I believe in God and times when I don't."

"Tell me about the times you don't believe in Him."

"When he sends sickness, suffering, and death. When he sends lightning to strike my barn and floods to wash away my crops. When he sends war."

"My word! If that is the kind of God you have, it is no wonder that your children get mumps, chicken pox, and polio, that the family gets the flu, that something is always out of joint. The thing you greatly fear does come upon you."

2.

One evening after a lecture a member of my congregation said to me, "I was born during the depression and I can never hope to be prosperous. Everything I do turns out bad."

"Oh, please," I said, "think of what you are doing to yourself, to your mind, and to your affairs. Don't you realize that men are like the God they worship? If that is the kind of a God you have, how can you hope to be prosperous? How can you hope to be well? How can you hope to be anything that is worthwhile?"

He didn't hear God's question, *"Believe ye that I am able to do this?"* But if he had, this would have been his answer, "No, Lord, I don't believe because I was born under an unlucky sign. I was born during a panic."

The Lord's response would certainly have been something like this: "I can do no mighty works here because of his unbelief. He isn't worshipping Me. He is worshipping a depression."

3.

"Believe ye that I am able to do this?" I repeat the demand that Jesus made.

"Well, let me think a moment. I am not just sure, says the person on the other side of the desk.

"But you are told that *'God is able to do for you exceeding abundantly above all that you ask or think.'* "

"That's true, but you see I haven't had very much experience."

"Then get some. What is your God able to do for you? I mean what are you able to conceive of Him doing?"

"Well, He is able to heal a cut. I have had that experience. He is able to heal a headache. He is able to find a parking place for me. He is able to sell Life Insurance through me. He is able to harmonize a broken friendship. He is able to find a lost ring."

"But hold on for just a moment. There is only One Presence and Power in the Universe. If you have the consciousness of Truth, cancer, polio, multiple sclerosis, strokes, and other things that frighten the wits out of people are healed as readily as the cut and the headache."

"Believe ye that I am able to do this?" He demands of you.

Commit yourself. Take a stand. The healing is ready to take place, but its appearance depends upon whether you are on a material or a spiritual basis. Yes, I know how many times you have failed. But this is different. The Master is speaking to you now. What are you thinking? What are you feeling? What are you saying? What are you believing? Have you forgotten that you cannot follow two beliefs and get one result? Why have you not been healed? Why have your treatments failed? Because deep down in the submerged depths of your being, you did not believe.

Are you in the Law? Are you in Life? Then anything you ask *"believing,"* you shall have. Does than mean hypertension?

Does it mean high blood pressure, heart trouble, tuberculosis, cerebral palsy? What does Jesus say? *"If ye shall ask anything in my name* [anything you ask in consciousness], *I will do it."* Answer me. Do you know in Whom you believe? Are you persuaded that He is able to keep that which you have committed unto Him?

Then get your trolley back on the wire. Keep yourself on the beam. Stop criticizing people. Stop being resentful, querulous, suspicious, and anxious. Be your Best Self. When you make a claim on the Universe, back it up with your consciousness. Stay with it as Jacob did with his angel; *"I will not let you go until you bless me."*

There are many people who are still carrying unsolved problems and unfulfilled desires, simply because they have not wrestled with their angel (unknown self). Job was utterly defeated and flat on his back. Do you remember that he said, "Though He slay me, yet will I trust in Him"? We need some of that bulldog tenacity in our lives, too. "I will not let you go until you bless me. [I will not recant. I will not give up.]" Are you blocking your good with interference from the lower mind? Is there static in your consciousness?

"All power is given unto me in heaven and in earth." We have the power to heal, and we have the power to be healed. It doesn't matter one iota how the power comes nor through what factors it emerges.

As we said before, there are some people who not only discredit doctors and medicine but refuse to have anything to do with either one. Can it be that they forget that Jesus also used objective methods to arouse the patient's faith? Do they not know that medical science is an expression of Divine

Intelligence? Read the healing miracles in the New Testament and see how many times Jesus set His patients to doing things. On one occasion, He used mud on the eyes of a blind man. To the lepers, He said, *"Go show yourselves to the priests."* To Naaman, He said, *"Go wash in Jordan."* To the man sick of the palsy, He said, *"Arise, take up thy bed and walk."*

Is that any different from some of the prescriptions today? Go get a massage. Go out and play golf. Go down to the club and take a swim. Go to the Turkish Bath. Where is the therapy in these prescriptions? In the bath? In the swimming pool? On the golf course? The therapy is in the faith the patient has in a method. When we understand the principle of spiritual healing, we shall see that the Power works through the doctor just as it does through the practitioner and that whatever lifts the patient's consciousness is good therapy. Did not Jesus use suggestion in the case of Nicodemus and use telepathy in the cases of Jairus' daughter and the centurion's servant?

Did He need clay in order to heal blindness? Certainly not. He used clay because of the way the blind man's faith worked.

Jesus said, *"Thy sins be forgiven thee* [the sin of doubt, the sin of fear, the sin of frustration, the sin of defeat, the sin of confusion]." Sin is anything in the consciousness which contradicts, confuses, divides, separates, or defeats us. *"Believe ye that I am able to do this?"* *"Yea, Lord, I believe."*

Sin and disease are not causes; they are effects. Jesus said; "My Kingdom is not of this world." Then why do you persist in viewing conditions from the material or mental standpoint? Is it any wonder that you fail to bring about healings? *"My Kingdom"* is a spiritual Kingdom. That means that you are working on the Higher Plane—the Plane of *"Whereas before*

I was blind, now I see." See what? See that God is the only Reality. See that which is permanent. See that which in unconditioned. See that which is eternally perfect. See that which is unchangeable. See that which is real. See that disease exists only on the relative plane — the plane on which the earth was once believed to be flat.

Just as a generator steps down electricity and makes it available to man, so the awareness of Truth brings God into every situation. We have read and talked enough about God. What we need now is the realization of the I-AM-NESS of Christ. Healing does not come through correcting and adjusting things in the mind, body, or affairs; it comes through the consciousness of the Presence of Christ. By abiding in the Truth, we unerringly dissolve troublesome thoughts and conditions.

The way we react to disease, diagnosis, prognosis, and the erroneous claims of the race mind determines conditions in our lives. We are not hurt by anything in the outer world but by our reactions to its claims. We must believe in a power within us, not over us. The power to cause suffering is in our reaction.

Are you seeking healing for yourself or for another? Do you consider the illness serious? Do you believe that it requires skilled attention? Do you accept the opinion that there is something to be adjusted, destroyed, removed, or overcome? If you are giving power to material conditions even while you call upon the therapy of an Unconditioned Power, the healing will be delayed. You are treating in a divided consciousness. You are trying to see in two directions at the same time. You are affirming the Divine Presence and denying It in the same breath. What is needed to heal any condition is consciousness of Oneness with God. When the treatment touches the Presence, the condition is healed.

"But what shall I do when the appearance of the discord returns to my thought?" you ask. Refuse to react to it. That is what Jesus meant when He said *"put up thy sword."* Stop combatting evil. *"Agree with thine adversary quickly while thou art in the way with him."* The best way to agree with an adversary is to refuse to react to him. When you stop fighting or resisting a condition, you are withdrawing the very substance and power upon which it feeds, and it will soon pass away. The moment you realize that there is no power outside of you that has power to inflict evil on you, you have taken a tremendous step forward.

When the metaphysician says that disease is unreal, he does not mean that it has no existence but that it is impermanent. Disease comes and goes. It is unreal in that it has no mind, law, power, or substance to sustain it.

Now check yourself at this point. How do you really think of disease? If you view it from the three-dimensional (material) plane, you will think that it is real. The church is still trying to save sinners, trying to save souls, trying to beat down Satan. The surgeons are trying to cut out disease. (And God bless them! They are doing a good job on that plane!) But this is the world of effects.

Jesus said, *"I and the Father ·are one."* In this Oneness is the answer to every problem, the healing of every disease, the fulfillment of every desire. The awareness -of this Oneness makes us independent of people, circumstances, and conditions.

Do you see how important your outlook is? If disease is real, it cannot be healed by any body, in any way, on any plane.

Healers of every kind might just as well close up shop. But if disease is an illusion, a false belief, an erroneous concept of life, it can be transcended and dissolved by a consciousness of Truth.

Then how will you tackle disease? Well, if you are wise you won't tackle it at all. If you do, you will be defeated before you start. Just as soon as you admit that there is a diseased condition to be healed, you are working from effect to cause — you are putting the cart before the horse. You are admitting that disease is real and unreal at the same time and also recognizing that somebody has to do something about it. In other words, you are in the same position as the doctor whose kingdom of activity is in this world. Yes, that is true. You have assumed the Presence and denying It in the same breath. What is needed to heal any condition is consciousness of Oneness with God. When the treatment touches the Presence, the condition is healed.

"But what shall I do when the appearance of the discord returns to my thought?" you ask. Refuse to react to it. That is what Jesus meant when He said *"put up thy sword."* Stop combatting evil. *"Agree with thine adversary quickly while thou art in the way with him."* The best way to agree with an adversary is to refuse to react to him. When you stop fighting or resisting a condition, you are withdrawing the very substance and power upon which it feeds, and it will soon pass away. The moment you realize that there is no power outside of you that has power to inflict evil on you, you have taken a tremendous step forward.

When the metaphysician says that disease is unreal, he does not mean that it has no existence but that it is impermanent. Disease comes and goes. It is unreal in that it has no mind, law, power, or substance to sustain it.

Now check yourself at this point. How do you really think of disease? If you view it from the three-dimensional (material) plane, you will think that it is real. The church is still trying to save sinners, trying to save souls, trying to beat down Satan. The surgeons are trying to cut out disease. (And God bless them! They are doing a good job on that plane!) But this is the world of effects.

Jesus said, *"I and the Father are one."* In this Oneness is the answer to every problem, the healing of every disease, the fulfillment of every desire. The awareness of this Oneness makes us independent of people, circumstances, and conditions.

Do you see how important your outlook is? If disease is real, it cannot be healed by any body, in any way, on any plane. Healers of every kind might just as well close up shop. But if disease is an illusion, a false belief, an erroneous concept of life, it can be transcended and dissolved by a consciousness of Truth.

Then how will you tackle disease? Well, if you are wise you won't tackle it at all. If you do, you will be defeated before you start. Just as soon as you admit that there is a diseased condition to be healed, you are working from effect to cause — you are putting the cart before the horse. You are admitting that disease is real and unreal at the same time and also recognizing that somebody has to do something about it. In other words, you are in the same position as the doctor whose kingdom of activity is in this world. Yes, that is true. You have assumed the same relation to the diseased person as the doctor who attends him. You have traded a spiritual belief for a material belief, and you might just as well give up.

There is nothing to be destroyed, dissolved, set aside, or overcome. There is only a condition to be fulfilled — *"I live: yet not I, but Christ liveth in me."* "But I have said that hundreds of times," you say, "and nothing has ever come of it." Nothing does come unless your words have the consciousness to back them up, unless you feel the Christ at the Center of your being. Do you run for the medicine bottle when you are ill or do you instantly realize, *"I and the Father are one"*?

It is very easy to repeat the words, *"I and the Father are one,"* but the mere repetition of the statement does not make it true even though it is. You must also have a consciousness of your Oneness. You must have a realization of it. We have sickness and suffering because of our belief in a life separate and apart from God.

God is the only Cause; the only thing Principle can create is good. Where is the trouble then? In our reactions to material conditions, in our belief that there is a power apart from God.

The treatment for any difficulty, obstacle, or problem is to know this truth: "God is my instant and unfailing Supply." That is all you need. Just those seven words and the consciousness of Truth to back them up. Are you one of those who try to use Principle to demonstrate over difficulties and problems? The right way is to let Principle use you. Why? Because God is Principle and God cannot be used. Actually the only thing you have to do in practice is to provide the proper conditions through which the Divine Presence can manifest Itself. Approaching your problems from this angle insures the success of your demonstration.

What do we mean by the term, *demonstration?* A demonstration is the materialization of an idea or the fulfillment of a desire.

It is a revelation on the relative plane of that which is already in Mind.

Treatment for Healing

"I am come that they might have life and have it more abundantly."

"The words that I speak unto you, they are spirit and they are life."

I now renounce any belief that I am bound by the limitations of my physical body. I realize that the Abundant Life is one of wholeness, perfection, and beauty. I claim this life as my own.

I see the Spiritual Man that I AM, for I know that *"I and the Father are one."* In this Oneness, there can be no lack, no shortage, no deficiency, no imperfection. There is only wholeness, completeness, integration, unity.

I lift my consciousness above the level of my problem and see it dissolve into its native nothingness. *"In Him, I live and move and have my being."*

I now am established in health, in peace, in prosperity, in joy. I accept these blessings with gratitude. I accept the responsibilities they entail.

I know what I want in this specific demonstration. (State is clearly.) I have faith that God is able to grant this request. I have faith in myself as a medium through which His Power and Perfection can and will express.

I relax from all tension, effort, and strain.

I ask and accept forgiveness for all my mistakes in thought and action. I freely forgive those who in any way have injured or attempted to injure me. I sense the consciousness in which there is nothing to forgive, for I see the Spiritual Self in each one of us — the Perfect Self.

I speak, believing that I have received at this very instant the good that I seek. Amen.

Chapter VII
Try Faith in Prosperity

The keys to the Kingdom of Heaven were given to faith, which can unlock any door. The fulfillment of all desires is given to faith. Fences are torn down, walls crumble, and doors spring open under its power. When we hold steadfastly to the fulfillment of our desire, the Law of Faith establishes it as a reality in our lives.

Prosperity is already a part of our nature. If we are not experiencing abundance, we are holding wrong states of thought. We are, so to speak, standing in our own light. Our faith is working against our best interests instead of for them.

God does not withhold anything from us. But we withhold good from ourselves through our lack of awareness and understanding.

Do you see why it is necessary to change your point of view? As God's sons, we are entitled to all that God has. It may take time to get this realization, but we must work on it until it comes. Read the words of the prophet Haggai: *"The silver is mine, and the gold is mine, saith Jehovah of hosts."* Everything in the world belongs to God and is held by Him until we claim our oneness with the Lord (Law). When we are wrestling with financial difficulties, it is hard for us to accept the fact that we have to get on to a spiritual basis and change our perspective.

Robert A. Russell

Robert Browning said:

> "Truth is within ourselves; it takes no rise
> From outward things, whate'er you may believe.
> There is an inmost centre in us all,
> Where truth abides in fulness; . . . . . .
> . . . . and to know
> Rather consists in opening a way out
> Whence the imprisoned splendor may escape,
> Than in effecting entry for a light
> Supposed to be without."

The place to appropriate Divine Substance is within the consciousness. Our lack of faith, awareness, and understanding is the only obstacle that can restrict or prevent its expression. There is no limit to Divine Substance but the limit we place upon it in our thoughts and beliefs. It flows through us and our affairs according to the degree of our acceptance of it. The capacity of our faith is determined by the quality of our thinking.

Faith is a state or quality of mind which may be used for good or ill, for success or failure, for prosperity or poverty. Used negatively or against our best interests, it becomes fear or, as we say in metaphysics, faith in evil.

Every decision we make and everything we do are acts of faith. We have at this moment all the faith there is. Our responsibility is to choose how it shall be used. Rich is he who uses it in the right way!

Positive faith is the belief that we have the power, through God, to accomplish all things. It brings more of everything good to those who cultivate it. It is a mighty magnet that draws from Mind Substance the fulfillment of every right desire. *"By faith Enoch was translated that he should not see death . . . . By faith Noah . . . . . prepared an ark to the saving of his house . . . . . . .B y faith Abraham, when he was tried, offered up Isaac . . . . By faith Moses, when he was born, was hid three months of his parents . . . . By faith the walls of Jericho fell down . . . . And what shall I say more? for the time would fail me if I tell of Gideon, and of Barak, and of Samson and of Jephthah; of David also, and Samuel, and of the prophets; who through faith subdued kingdoms, wrought righteousness, obtained promises, stopped the mouths of lions, quenched the violence of fire, escaped the edge of the sword, out of weakness were made strong, waxed valiant in fight, turned to flight the armies of aliens."*

Jesus understood the negative and positive aspects of faith. He said, *"Whosoever . . . . . shall not doubt in his heart, but shall believe that those things which he saith shall come to pass; he shall have whatsoever he saith."* When a man thinks within himself, "I never get any breaks. Everyone takes advantage of me. I was born under an unlucky star. Nobody wants me. I am a misfit. I never get any opportunities" and believes that what he says is true, these conditions will certainly exist in his life until he changes his belief.

Stop right now and ask yourself how you have been using your faith. Think for a moment about your thoughts, beliefs, attitudes, and conversation. Have they been representative of what you would like to see materialized in your life? Have they given evidence of your awareness of the Source of Supply?

Since faith plays such a vital part in all creative activities, we must make sure that our faith is positive. The poor man does not need more faith but needs to redirect the faith he now has. Many men have dreamed dreams and imagined wonderful things who lacked the faith to bring them into being. The dreamer has his place in the scheme of things, but dreams without faith are futile.

Possibilities become tangible only through faith. Man may have great plans but without faith in his ability to put the plans into operation, the plans die. James Freeman Clark once said, "All the strength and force of man comes from his faith in things unseen. He who believes is strong; he who · doubts is weak. Strong convictions precede great actions. The man strongly possessed of an idea is the master of all who are uncertain or wavering. Clean, deep, living convictions rule the world."

Once we have perceived God as our supply and have convinced the personal self that this is true, prosperity will come as naturally as the rising of the sun. When Jesus said, *"Whatsoever things ye desire, when ye pray believe that ye have received them and ye shall have them,"* He was telling us that there is no space between the idea of good and the consciousness that supplies it because the idea is in Mind.

In demonstrating prosperity, we are dealing with ideas and not money. Vivian May Williams says, "God has nothing to give you but ideas, and these ideas are your sustenance and support, for you are a Spiritual (mental) being, and therefore nothing can nourish you but ideas. Since you are mind and not body, the consciousness of an idea is equivalent to receiving the thing itself, for all God's ideas are things in reality."

We speak of Mind as the only actor in the universe but we know that It acts on ideas and ideas are crystalized and clarified through words. Holding the right words in mind until they form a consciousness of themselves gradually develops a subjective conviction that enables to say *"All things that the Father hath are mine."*

Prosperity means different things to different people. What does it mean to you? What do you see, what do you feel when you speak the word? Clarify your idea by making a list of the things you would do and the things you would have if you had great prosperity. See yourself using all this abundance and wealth. Activate your faith by keeping this vision before your mind. Believe that God wishes you to be prosperous. Believe that your desire is fulfilled now. Study the things in the New Testament that Jesus said about money.

Know, however, that you cannot go beyond your mental equivalent. If you desire an abundance of money and have a subconscious pattern of $75.00 a week, you will find yourself in the seventy-five dollar class. The subjective pattern is always more powerful than the conscious demand. Those who have continuous prosperity have established a habit of prosperity. Prosperity habits can be stored away in the subconscious mind like reserve funds in the bank. The people who have plenty of money are the people who do not have to think about money. They have a subjective conviction that they will always have plenty of money and they do. Their conviction has created a subconscious pattern in their Jives. The poor man, on the other hand, has no conviction about Universal Supply. Believing that money. depends upon the sweat of his brow, he limits his capacity for making money to this one means.

The materialist thinks that there is a limit to God's abundance; the metaphysician knows that it is inexhaustible and always asks for all the money he can use.

Demonstrating prosperity is like demonstrating anything else. We must follow the rules to secure results. If we are not satisfied with what we are getting out of life, we must find out where we are falling down. We must examine ourselves.

The answer is not in the outside world but within us. We are limited in supply only because we are limited in our beliefs. The Principle of Prosperity will have no limit in our experience when we learn how to accept and use It. To get big dividends, we must make the right investments.

1. WE MUST LEARN HOW TO INCREASE OUR FAITH.

Many people start out on a spiritual project with the purpose of increasing faith as though It could be pumped up like a balloon. The way to. make faith grow is to put into action that faith. we already have. When we put faith to work In the right way, we find that it is limitless. Faith is one of those rare and priceless possessions that no one can borrow, buy, beg, or steal from us. It is something that no one can give us. "But my faith is so inadequate," you say. Then develop it. The moment we understand that All-Faith is individualized in each one of us, we begin to see that the possibility of experiencing abundance is limitless. Back of every fortune and success is faith. Once we have established it, growth and prosperity are inevitable.

2. WE MUST SEE MONEY FOR WHAT IT IS.

Money is only the symbol of our ability to express beauty and order and comfort in our lives. It is one of the many external evidences that we have established our unity with the Source of all Good, with the Universal Creator. Prosperity is an outward and visible sign of an inward and spiritual grace . . . . . the belief in a loving and all-powerful Father. Rising above a sense of lack is consistent with the breaking down of other limitations and the complete acceptance of freedom from anything that hinders the operation of the Divine Law in our lives.

If we think of prosperity in terms of dollars, we have an erroneous concept. Money is a basic part of our economic system, but dollars are merely the medium through which supply comes. If there were no money, there would still be bread, beans, eggs, cattle, automobiles, houses, and land. The medium is not important. If we have the consciousness of prosperity, we shall have lots of bread, beans, eggs, houses, land, dollars, or whatever the medium of exchange happens to be. When we realize that our consciousness is the substance of all form, we shall no longer depend upon material dollars but upon spiritual ideas. The reality of money is not in dollars but in consciousness. Jesus' statement, *"Whosoever will lose his life for my sake shall find it,"* applies to money, too. He who loses the false sense of material dollars will find plenty of dollars.

Many persons think that money comes only from time spent at labor. But there are many business executives and others who do very little work and yet draw huge salaries. They take vacations two or three times a year and do pretty much as they please. Do these men draw tremendous salaries because of the number of hours they work? By no means. They are convinced that they are worth that much and they get it.

Money is a spiritual thing, otherwise Jesus would not have taught us to pray, *"Thy Kingdom come. Thy Will be done on earth."* The truth. Is that Jesus said more about money than He did about Heaven. Indeed, it is one of the mediums through which God's purposes are worked out. Jesus never condemned riches as such nor condemned any man because he was rich.

There are still people who believe that money is evil, but they go right on working for it and using it. The evil, you see, is in their beliefs or in the unworthy ends to which money is often put and not in the money itself.

Just as good circulation is necessary for the health of the body, so good circulation is necessary to prosperity, in our bank accounts, pocketbooks, and in our mental attitude toward money.

How, then, shall we increase the circulation of money in our affairs? By loving money for the good we can do with it. What we love increases. When we think of money as the means God uses to maintain a circulation in our affairs, our supply will increase. Let us be careful, however, about hoarding money or damming it up. The moment we fence it in, we violate one of the basic laws of prosperity.

David sang, *"The earth is the Lord's and the fulness thereof, the world and they that dwell therein."* Think of that for a few minutes, and you will see that we do not own anything, not even our lives. We are only stewards of money, holding it for a brief moment, and then giving an account as to how it was used.

Do you remember what Jesus said to the man who thought he owned all the stuff he had acquired? *"Thou fool, this night thy soul shall be required of thee: then whose shall these things be, which thou hast provided?"* The answer to this question is in the free-for-all which so often follows the reading of a will or settlement of an estate. How proudly some people boast of the possessions they have amassed! They act as though they were going to live on this earth forever. It never occurs to them that all they have will some day pass into other hands.

Perhaps we should remind ourselves at least once a day that our business is God's Business and that our money is God's Money. What a difference it would make in our income if we could get a sense of God in our job, profession, or business; if we could write over every farm house, doctor's office, mercantile company, law firm, court room, dry goods store, hospital, laboratory, filling station, factory and mill, "God's Business"; if every owner or worker would say, "I am in business with God." When we bring God into our business, it becomes God's Business.

We claim to have but one God. Yet our conduct, conversation, and behavior often proclaim many gods. Whatever we ascribe power to becomes a god to us. We should remember this when we are tempted to give power to depression, limitation, unemployment, and hard times. The secret of an enduring prosperity is not only to attune ourselves to the Divine Source, but to acknowledge It constantly in gratitude and faith, leaving it to God to create the channels through which the streams of abundance flow into our lives. The ability to attract money is as much a spiritual gift as the ability to translate the Bible.

3. WE MUST REALIZE THE RECIPROCAL RELATIONSHIP OF GIVING AND GETTING.

Some years ago, an astonishing article in one of the great newspapers of Detroit told of a number of persons who had gained great wealth because the farms which had belonged to their parents or grandparents had become valuable sub-division property which had yielded them fortunes. Then it told of what had happened to a great number of these persons. One tragedy after another had resulted directly from the unwise use of their money. Gross immorality, divorces, crime, and insanity had entered into the lives of many of those who had come into possession of large wealth for which they had rendered no corresponding service to the world.

Roger Babson says: "If things are not going well with you, begin your effort at correcting the situation by carefully examining the service you are rendering, and especially the spirit in which you are rendering it." This is particularly good advice for one seeking to demonstrate prosperity. It doesn't make any. difference what kind of service you may be giving — tailoring, dressmaking, typing, bookkeeping, selling, plumbing, reading meters, servicing cars, banking, binding books, printing, or preaching sermons, the important thing is the spirit in which it is rendered. Trying to acquire wealth without giving service is self-defeating.

Money gained by gambling, crooked deals, shady practices, dishonesty, and theft brings sorrow, frustration, and disappointment, for no service has been rendered for the money acquired. Inherited wealth often brings quarreling, trickery, and unhappiness with it because nothing has been done to earn it and plans for its use are self-centered. If there is no vision or plan for worthwhile service in inherited wealth, it quickly disintegrates.

There are persons who make pledges of money to churches and other worthy causes and fail to fulfill them, and yet these pledges are promises, or covenants, or contracts. Does anyone think that money saved or withheld in such a manner benefits him? Doesn't he realize that in the course of time he will lose the amount of the unpaid pledge in some unexpected and unforeseen way? Thousands of people can testify that by this kind of failure they have lost the amount withheld and more through means they had not dreamed of.

A man may be ever so proficient in prayer, meditation, practice, and knowledge. He may know the Bible from cover to cover. He may be well-versed in metaphysics, mental science and psychology. He may know the Law, Truth, and Principle. But if he fails to serve mankind, gives grudging half-hearted service, or is selective in his service, he cannot prosper. Solomon said long ago, *"In all thy ways acknowledge*

Him, and he shall direct thy paths." Jesus said, *"Inasmuch as ye have done it unto one of the least of these my brethren, ye have done it unto me."*

George Herbert gave us four lines that tell the story:

> "A servant with this clause
>> Makes drudgery divine;
> Who sweeps a room as for Thy laws
>> Makes that and th' action fine."

4.   WE MUST FORGIVE OUR DEBTORS.

We can never be prosperous and free until we have forgiven everybody for everything we hold against them. Before good can flow *toward* us, it must first flow *from* us.

Do you remember what Jesus said about the acceptability of a sacrifice? *"Leave there thy gift before the altar, and go thy way; first be reconciled to thy brother, and then come and offer thy gift."* On another occasion, He said, *"When ye stand praying, forgive, if ye have ought against any: that your Father also which is in Heaven may forgive you your trespasses. But. if ye do not forgive, neither will your Father which is in Heaven forgive your trespasses."*

According to Webster, the word *forgive* means "To give up resentment against another because of wrong committed; to give up any claim which we may have against another; to absolve; to pardon." In Aramic, the word forgive means to release and set free from bondage. When we refuse to forgive another for some fancied or real hurt, we not only bind him but we also fetter ourselves.

Because Jesus knew how difficult it is to nullify revengeful and destructive attitudes and feelings, He said to *"forgive seventy times seven"* times. Multiply seventy by seven and we have four hundred and ninety. Not many of us need to go this far with forgiveness because we usually flush the resentment out before we reach the first ten.

5. WE MUST HAVE THE MENTAL EQUIVALENT OF THAT FOR WHICH WE PRAY.

Remembering that wealth is a relative thing, we should never pray for a specific sum of money. We should specify our need, the purpose to which what we pray for is to be put, or the effect we want it to have. We should think in terms of abundance and of the relationship of our desire to greater freedom, increased livingness, and fuller expression of life.

No understanding person desires money for money's sake. He sees in it a means to happiness, freedom, independence, contentment, peace of mind, and ability to help and serve others.

We should preface every claim with the words, "I AM," strongly accented. Jesus said, "Before Abraham was, *I AM*." St. James said, *"Every good gift and every perfect gift is from above, and cometh down from the Father of lights with whom is no variableness, neither shadow of turning."* ["The good and perfect gift already exists though unseen."] We cannot create prosperity by working, begging, worrying, striving, or thinking. The Finished Kingdom is not taken by violence but by recognition and acceptance. When the little self is raised to the understanding of the "I AM," or the Truth of the Real Self, the mere wish for a thing will draw it to us. If God is All-Good and we are one with God, everything we desire is ours now.

Are you ready now to demonstrate prosperity through the power of your faith? Having cultivated the ground, it is time to plant the seed. Your desire is for greater prosperity; God knows how to bring it to you. You are dealing with Law; Law knows how to provide what you need and also how to furnish the channels through which it shall come. Since this has been explained step by step in great detail in a previous book, *You, Too, Can Be Prosperous,* only a brief outline is given here.

In all spiritual therapy, work should be done in the Silence. Approach the treatment through the following steps:

1. Believe that there is nothing too great for God to give you. *"God is able to make all grace abound toward you; that ye, always having all sufficiency in all things, may abound to every good work."*

2. Believe that you are attracting a prosperity which is commensurate with the unlimited and inexhaustible riches of Spirit. *"Then shalt thou lay up gold as dust, and the gold of Ophir as the stones of the brooks."*

3. Believe that this prosperity already exists for you. *"It is your Father's good pleasure to give you the Kingdom."*

4. Believe that it is yours by right of consciousness according to the promise, *"And my God shall supply all your needs according to His riches in Christ Jesus in glory."*

5. Believe that what you ask for has already been given you. *"What things soever ye desire, when ye pray, believe that ye have received them, and ye shall have them."*

6. Believe that money is flowing to you from every direction. *"According to your faith, be it unto you."*

Treatment for Prosperity

In the stillness of the Silence, I open my mind and heart to the Divine Substance of Spirit. I acknowledge God as the Source of All Supply. I cleanse my subconscious mind of everything that would prevent me from recognizing my right to all good. I empty it of every thought of lack, limitation, and poverty and give my whole mind over to the thought of the Abundance of God. I feel this Substance pressing against my consciousness for expression as I recall His promise: *"Before they call, I will answer"* My whole being is aware of the outpouring of His riches. I know that the fulfillment of my desire for prosperity will be demonstrated without delay. I know that the supply I ask in prayer, believing, I shall receive. My supply is here now. It is within me and around me; it flows to me from every direction. It comes to me wherever I am and in whatever I do. My supply is instant and unfailing. I am richly endowed with an abundance of everything good.

I accept this prosperity now. I identify all my enterprises, activities, and plans with success. I think according to Principle and accept abundance in every form. Whatever I need is wherever I am. I no longer see lack, limitation, or poverty. I claim the All-Sufficiency of God. I am one with God and His wealth. Wealth fills my purse, my bank account, my life, my home, my business, and my world. I use the money I have wisely, release it in faith, and know that it will return to me, pressed down, shaken together, and running over.

Chapter VIII
Try Making a Personal Check-Up

When the car doesn't perform properly, we take it to the garage for a check-up. When some part of the body fails to function, we go to the doctor for an examination. When our consciousness works against our best interests, we should analyze our beliefs, thoughts, attitudes, and mental habits.

Let us test ourselves by self-examination. Let us check ourselves against the rules. Let us find out where we are falling down so we may know what to do to get better results.

As you read, ask yourself the question that leads each section, and answer in terms of the discussion that follows.

1. CHECK THE SOURCE.

Do I know where my supply comes from?

Most people approach their problems from the wrong end. The Good we are seeking comes not from the outer world but from within. *"THE KINGDOM OF GOD"* said Jesus *"IS WITHIN YOU."* We are focal points of Its expression. Good first exists within us. We have only to change our consciousness to allow It to be expressed in our living. It will materialize in our experience when we remove the obstacles It encounters.

Since God is the Creative Source, to take the credit for our supply because of what we do a the job, business, or profession, or to give the credit for our health to our heredity or to observance of rules, is to deny the Creative Principle — to take credit for something that doesn't belong to us. Perhaps that is the reason we sometimes have a difficult time in contacting the Source when we are in need. If we do not acknowledge God as the Source of our Supply in periods of health, peace, and prosperity, we cannot expect to find Him quickly in time of need. To believe that our good is dependent upon personality severs our connection with the actual Source.

If we want to find the Source of all Good, we must reach back through the self to the Divine Substance and Life of which we are a part and realize our oneness with it.

THE LAW OF FAITH ACTING THROUGH THOUGHT INCREASES OR RETARDS THE FLOW OF SUBSTANCE.

Make sure that you understand this point before going to the next one. Your success in demonstrating prosperity or anything else you desire is determined by the level of your understanding of this statement.

You are a thinking center of Divine Mind. Substance flows through you and for you according to your faith. If you have been using the Law of Faith negatively, drawing lack, limitation, disease, and failure into your experience, you can change these manifestations by changing your thought. Do you see the picture? Do you understand it? When you change your consciousness out of a negative state into a positive state, you reverse the Law and change its expression in your life. Instead of working against you, the Law of Faith works with you.

The Law of Attraction on any plane is stated in the Master's words, *"I and the Father are one,"* Get this understanding and you need not fight, worry, or struggle for your good. Wherever you are, the Allness of God is. This makes you independent of money, people, circumstance, conditions, and things. You are in the world but not of it. In this unity is your completeness, sustenance, wealth, support, and economic freedom. *"Happy is the man,"* said Solomon, *"that findeth wisdom and the man that getteth understanding, for the merchandise of it is better than the merchandise of silver, and the gain thereof than fine gold."*

Solomon did not lean upon the perishable symbol of dollars and cents but upon the imperishable and invisible ideas in mind, and so must we.

2. CHECK YOUR EMOTIONS.

What do I do about fear?

If you are suffering from ill health, unhappiness, or financial stringency at the present time, it is almost certain that you are also suffering from fear. Fear is faith working for the wrong thing. Fear and lack go hand in hand; you seldom find one without the other. Jesus said, *"According to your faith be it unto you."*

Faith works just as effectively for poverty as for prosperity, for health as disease, for peace as discord. Fear can be the most dangerous of all our emotions. Faith is a feeling and a conviction, an acceptance of an idea as real, whether it be positive or negative. What you fear, you have faith in and claim as your own. It you fear that some dreadful thing is going to happen to you, you have faith in evil and are attracting it to yourself.

Do you remember what Job said about his misadventures? *"That which I greatly feared has come upon me."* Had he been living in this time, he probably would have said, "All the evil that I saw and feared has settled down upon me."

Fear is the most creative of all the negative states of mind. Since the universe reacts according to our faith, a negative faith will always bring out the worst, not because we have consciously chosen it but because our faith is turned in the wrong direction.

Pessimistic moods—the feeling that everything seems to go wrong, worry over expense, dissatisfaction with the job, disappointment in some one dear, a sudden lack of self-confidence—are the common lot, but these moods require immediate and drastic handling by the seeker after Truth. Was there ever a year when spring did not come? Well, spring is here now if you wish it to be, for the weather in your mind is determined by your thoughts.

Life responds to us according to our expectations. Faith works for misfortune just as readily as it does for good fortune. To get the most out of life, we must keep our thought patterns positive. We must keep our emotions true. We must keep our faith moving in the right direction. If we have a negative faith, we must move it into positive channels. The law of reversal is very simple: Control your thinking.

3. Check Your Mental Images.

Do my mental images correspond to my desire?

In any demonstration, we must have a clear mental picture of what we want and then hold to that picture until it is established as a reality in our lives.

The imaging faculty (imagination) is the drafting department of the mind. We use it to make a clear and distinct picture of our desire. If we hold one picture today and another picture tomorrow, we run into a dead-end street. We are like the man of whom the Bible speaks: *"Let a man ask in faith, nothing wavering, for he who wavereth is like a wave of the sea, driven by the winds and tossed. Let not that man think he will receive anything good of the Lord."* Changing the picture from day to day ends in distortion. By holding the image steadfastly in thought, we give the Law of Faith a chance to establish it in our lives. We have the power to move in either direction; it takes no more power to move toward our goal than to move away from it. When we learn to identify ourselves with abundance and wealth (well-being), our affairs will reflect our prosperous state of mind.

4. CHECK YOUR RELATIONSHIP TO THE LAW.

How do I use the Law?

Everything that comes into our lives, whether good or ill, comes through Law. There is only one Law, but there are many ways of using it. The Law does not change; it cannot be abrogated, violated, nor set aside. To get good results in spiritual work, we must use the Law according to its nature; that is, the way it works. We must use it to bring out good instead evil. The Law does not know what we are using it for. It knows only how act. Moses said to the Children of Israel: *"Behold today I set before you a blessing or a curse."* We can use the Law to injure or to heal, to prosper or make poor. The effect of the Law is determined by our relationship to it. Shakespeare wisely said, "There is nothing either good or bad but thinking makes it so."

The Law increase whatever we give our attention to. Attention imparts substance and power to whatever it falls upon. If we constantly pay attention to our poverty, the poverty grows. By thinking about wealth, we activate the Principle of

Prosperity that gives form to the idea of substance and brings abundance into our affairs. By concentrating upon health, we make it a reality in our lives. The selection of the focus is our responsibility.

The Law is a doer but not a knower. It knows us only by what we know about ourselves. It can only follow the patterns that we give it. In fact, it is so exact that it works out every desire to the minutest detail. In the past, we have often use the Law to our detriment and produced bondage. Now we are able to use it to our advantage to produce freedom. Many people think of the Law as if it were two powers, but this is an erroneous concept. Good and evil are just two ways of using the one Life Force. Lack comes to us through the same Law that produces plenty. If we are tired of limited health, circumstances, and happiness, we must stop thinking and talking about them. If we have been using the Law in a limited way, we must now reverse the process and use it in an unlimited way. When we are rightly related to the Law—using it positively instead of negatively, our thought of abundance will produce plenty, our thought of wholeness will produce health, our realization of our Oneness with the Source will result in joy. We can determine our relationship to the Law by watching our spontaneous thought process.

5. CHECK YOUR HABITS.

Do my habits serve or frustrate me?

What a tremendous power habit is! It is God's way of making Good automatic in man's life. It is Nature's way of turning thought and action over to the subconscious mind. Man has the power of choice as to the direction of his thinking, the quality of his thought, and the mental habits he establishes.

Having chosen, he ceases to be responsible for the manner or the means by which his thought becomes reality. His subconscious takes over and reproduces in his life the pattern he has set up in his thinking.

William James said, "The more details of our life we can hand over to the effortless custody of habit, the more our higher forces of mind will be set free for their proper work." How important it is then to get our habits working for us instead of against us! How essential it is to deposit in the treasury of the subconscious mind impulses that produce good! When an idea becomes habitual, it materializes in our lives automatically.

Everyone should seek a consistent and persistent Good. There is no reason why we should alternate between health and illness, joy and grief, good seasons and bad seasons, financial ups and financial downs. If we are using the Principle according to its nature, we are established in peace, prosperity, and perfection.

6. CHECK YOUR SERVICE.

What kind of service do I give?

One of the Laws seldom stressed in metaphysical teachings is the Law of Service. It is a point of weakness in our work and probably draws more criticism than anything else. "You are too self-centered, too self-seeking," says the critic. We sometimes tend to forget that no other teaching of the Master falls with greater force upon the well-being of mankind than this matter of service. Wise indeed was the author of the motto: "He profits most who serves best." No Biblical promise is without a condition of some sort. The promise of prosperity — *"and all things shall be added unto you,"* is contingent upon our seeking the Kingdom first.

When we realize that our business is the "Father's Business," we shall carry His Spirit and Presence into every avenue and activity of our lives. We shall render our service, whether it be great or small, in the Spirit of the Master who said, *"I am among you as he that serveth."* We shall stop asking, "What are we going to get?" and shall ask, "What can we give?" We shall stop worrying about whether people appreciate us and learn to appreciate others. We shall recognize the love and power released in our lives as concomitants of the sincerity of our service.

To understand why so many people have ill health, financial difficulties, and discordant lives, it is only necessary to watch the indifferent service given to the public by many who earn their bread in a specific area. Real service is giving the best one has — whether it be helping someone on the street, showing courtesy to a stranger in a tax office, reciprocating a favor, answering a letter, or waiting on a customer. It is one of the laws that Jesus gave us: *"With what measure ye mete, it shall be measured to you again."*

7.   CHECK YOUR ATTITUDES TOWARD OTHERS.

What do I attract by my attitudes?

One of the psychic blocks that interfere with our demonstrations is indiscriminate criticism — seeing lack in others. Ill-will, animosity, and critical thought about other people seriously affect our own well-being. "What thou seest, that thou beest." What we see in others comes to dwell with us. If we see lack and express it, we attract lack. By such an attitude, we set in motion a law which repels our good instead of attracting it. Dwelling upon the limitations, mistakes, errors, shortcomings, and offenses of others results in materializing these shortages in our own lives. Vitriolic criticism is a form of destruction, retaliation, and revenge. But the way of God is forgiveness.

What the Law of Forgiveness really requires of us is that we turn our enemies and all those who offend us over to God. That is the first step in forgiving; it is accomplished by realizing that it is not the person that we resent or condemn but the particular- evil which is controlling him. Evil is never a part of any person; rather it is an iniquity that he has permitted to occupy his consciousness and control his actions. We are always dealing with a state of consciousness and not with a person.

The second step is to call the name of the person against whom we hold resentment or antagonism and declare: "By the love, power, and authority of Jesus Christ, I now forgive _____ for whatever he should be forgiven for." Then we should use the same words in forgiving ourselves for holding condemnation, bitterness, and revenge against the person we have named. In stubborn and deep rooted attitudes of vengeance and hate, we. may not have to forgive four hundred and ninety but we must keep at It until that part of our consciousness has been purified. What we are really doing in forgiving another is to remove the obstacles to the current of Divine Supply. The statement in the Lord's prayer, *"Forgive us our trespasses as we forgive those who trespass against us,"* means that our own claim to forgiveness depends upon our forgiveness of others.

There are other ways in which we can express forgiveness, such as praying for the offender, writing him a letter of good will saying as many nice things about him as we can, and meeting him on open, friendly terms.

8. Check Your Godliness.

Am I a godly man?

The Psalmist describes the godly man in the following words: *"But his delight is in the Law of the Lord; and in his law doth he meditate day and night. And he shall be like a tree planted by the rivers of water, that bringeth forth fruit in his season; his leaf also shall not wither and whatsoever he doeth shall prosper."*

The godly man is one who knows nothing but the Presence and Power of God in every person, place, and thing. He realizes that there is nothing but God in the universe and that he is God's activity. The godly man believes that he is a center through which the Universal Mind expresses Itself and that the measure of this expression depends upon his consciousness of It. Being one with God, he is like a tree planted by the rivers of water, drawing his supply from an invisible source which never fails. And how does the godly man draw upon this supply? By faith and acceptance. Knowing nothing but the Presence and Power of God in the universe, he attracts nothing but the good into his life and affairs. He becomes *"like a tree planted by the rivers of water . . . and whatsoever he doeth shall prosper."*

The godly man does not judge according to appearances but judges rather by righteous judgment. He does not think of God as handing out health and prosperity to a favored few and withholding these blessings from others. He knows that he is dealing with Law and not with a person and that this Law is to him what he is to It—that It reacts to him according to what he believes It to be. When things go wrong, the godly man does not blame persons, weather, circumstances, conditions, or God; he blames himself.

He knows that there is something between the Creative Process and his personal experience which is blocking the pathway of the Universal Intelligence and that it must be removed. How does he go about this? By substituting positive thought for the negative one.

The materialist on the other hand blames everybody and everything but himself. He sounds off like this: "Why didn't I get that job I so. much wanted? I suppose someone else had a bigger drag." "Why did I get fired? I'll bet the boss had a friend he wants to place." "Why did this deal fall through? The cards were stacked against me all the time." "Look at my peach trees. If God is the Source of my Supply and everywhere equally present, why did He allow this hail storm? Why did He allow the freeze?"

If you are guilty of such reactions, let me ask you a few questions. Did you ask God to express Himself through you and your affairs as supply? Did you take Him into partnership? Did you invoke divine protection?

If you are a gardener, a farmer, or a fruit grower, did you recognize and cooperate with the Life in the seeds you planted, or did you work against It? Planting crops or pruning fruit trees is just as much God's business as running a church or healing the sick. Or did you perhaps prevent God from expressing Himself in your affairs by surrounding your crops or fruit trees with fears about the weather, insects, and pests? What did you tell the Life in your seeds? What did you impress upon the fruit trees? Did you think or say or listen attentively to such ideas as these: "It is a cold spring, and I am afraid we are going to have a freeze." "We are getting too much rain." "We are not getting enough moisture." "It looks as if I'm going to have another failure."

If you are in business, did you cut yourself off from supply by resisting competition, by worrying about taxes, overhead, government control? By giving circumstances and conditions power over your success instead of placing your problems lovingly in God's Hands and depending upon His Law to promote and increase your prosperity and progress?

Are you a writer bemoaning the short story that the publishers rejected? Did you, from the beginning, place this story in God's Hands? Did you ask Him to think and write through you? Did you wait for His inspiration? Did you thank Him for each new Idea as it came? Did you ask Him to guide you to the right publishers when it was ready to be sent in, or did you send it where you thought you would get the largest check?

Since God is everywhere equally present, He is in every seed and in every idea as the Life Force that will produce all that we need when we recognize and cooperate with It. The godly man does not look to the weather or outside conditions when plowing his fields and planting his seeds. He looks only to God. He sees the Life in the seeds as containing everything needed for a perfect crop, including right growing weather and a good market. The godly man does not become gloomy and pessimistic when the barometer falls, for he knows that the Creative Law is operating for him and that It never fails. Knowing God, and God only, as the Source of his Supply, he can always say, "There is plenty more where this came from."

9. CHECK YOUR POINT OF VIEW.

Do I dwell in my Christ-Self or in my personality?

One of the first things the metaphysical student is taught is to claim that the good he desires is his now and to give thanks that he has it. How can we declare that we have a thing when there is no tangible evidence of it? This is hard to understand because we seem to be uttering a falsehood. There is an important principle involved in making such a claim.

When the metaphysician makes the statement that he has all things, he is not referring to the personality or "me" of himself, but to the "I" The "me" is only the skin-casing, as we might call it, under which is the True Self the invisible man, the perfect I AM which has always been. The metaphysician refers to this invisible man as the "undivided or unseparated self. There is a vast difference between the personality and the individuality. When we understand this distinction, we see that the "I," or true individual, is now and always has been one with the Father and can never be separated from Him. But the personality, the "me," or outer self, believes in two powers instead of one. It is that self of which St. Paul spoke when he said, *"put off the old man with his deeds."* Believing in separation from good, the "me" is the cause of all our trouble. Trying to serve the mind of the world instead of the *"mind which was in Christ Jesus,"* the "me" is serving the wrong master.

In most people, the personality "me" has been allowed to expand to such proportions that it has taken possession of the whole man. In fact, there are many people who think that the "me" is all there is of them. The true Being of man is the Christ, or I AM. Exalt this Self, and all things will be drawn to It until you express one whole, perfect, and complete being. Then you will understand" for the first time the meaning of the words, *"All things that the Father hath are mine."*

It is important to understand this. Since the higher self is always one with the Source of all Good, when I claim that the good I desire is mine now, I am speaking the Absolute Truth of my Christ-Self. How, then, do these things become literal in my experience? By convincing the "me" that the claim is justified. Until we get the true viewpoint, we shall continue to be sick and limited and will spend much of our time trying to demonstrate Truth.

When we switch from the "me and mine" consciousness to the "I and your" consciousness, the mere desire for a thing starts the working of the Law automatically. When you know that all things are yours in the "I" consciousness and you arrive at a subjective conviction of this Truth, thanking God for the fulfillment of your desire releases the Power that brings the desire into material form.

Now for a recapitulation. The first step in making a transition from the "me" to the "I" is to know that you are one with God and that all He has is yours. You must claim this with great feeling and conviction, not as the "me" but as the "I," which you are in Truth. The second step is to dwell upon this Truth until the "me" accepts it. See your desire in completion. Assume that the object of your desire is now in instant manifestation. Lift yourself to the consciousness wherein every desire you may ever have is already fulfilled. Let your prayer be one of joyous acceptance of the good that exists now in the Universe of Substance that is all around you.

Since the universe always accepts us at our · own evaluation, the important thing in time of need is to increase our consciousness of plenty, in time of illness to enlarge our concept of wholeness, in time of conflict to broaden our understanding of peace. When we enlarge our consciousness of good, good begins to move into our experience. We have whatever our consciousness is ready to receive. Our Supply is determined by the size of the cup we hold up.

Did you read thoughtfully? Did your vision grow? Did you get a glimpse of the new man that you can be? Are you determined now to enlarge the place of thy tent? Then try Practicing the Presence to this end.

Part Two

Chapter IX
Practicing the Presence of God

"And as they thus spake, Jesus himself stood in the midst of them, and saith unto them, Peace be unto you."

We know that God is both the highest God and the innermost God and that our minds are a part of His Mind. Thinking, therefore, is a two-fold process. We not only think with our own minds, but we also think in His Mind. For most of us, to think of Him as present in our own minds is the easiest way to conceive of the Presence and affords us the quickest way to contact Him. But the Presence is wherever we conceive Him to be. If we conceive Him to be in the Reserved Sacrament on the altar, He is there. If we think of Him as being present in illness, or danger, or disaster, He is there. If we conceive Him as with us in moments of triumph, elation, and happiness, He is there, too.

Because God is Omnipresent, we know Him to. be everywhere equally present. Being in our minds, He goes with us wherever we go and is instantly responsive to our every call. If we are lonely, He is at hand to comfort us. If we are in need, He is there to fulfill it. If we are sick, He is near to minister unto us. If we seek guidance, He gives it. Yes, the Christ is wherever we are at any and every moment, unseen by most of us, but just as present as when He walked the dusty roads of Capernaum and Galilee with Jesus.

Perhaps the greatest exponent of Practicing the Presence was Brother Lawrence of the middle ages. Like the mystics of all ages, he was a man of great faith and insight. Walking with God, he found Him even among the pots and pans of the kitchen where he worked as a cook.

His method was whole-hearted acceptance of the Christ as always and everywhere equally present. No matter what the circumstances or conditions were, the Living Presence was always there, meeting his smallest or his greatest need. To many persons, this will sound like a beautiful, visionary, and fantastic theory; but to those who practice this technique, it becomes an astonishing, practical, and vivid reality. Men and women in all walks of life, as well as great mystics such as Boehme, Eckhart, and Brother Lawrence, have found it to be fact and pot theory.

There is, standing beside, within, before, and behind each one of us, an invisible Presence. The New Testament calls this Presence Christ; the Old Testament calls it *Emmanuel* — a word meaning God-with-us. It was to this Presence that Jesus referred when He said, *"Greater is he that is in you than He that is in the world."* Regardless of what we call the Presence, It is that *"Light which lighteth every man that cometh into the world."* When the Light departs, the physical body begins to fall apart. Do you find this hard to believe? Then ask yourself these questions: Do eyes see? Do ears hear? Do brains think? Does the heart love? The answer is No. If eyes could see, ears hear, and brains think, they would go on seeing, hearing, and thinking forever.

Robert Browning referred to this Presence as the "imprisoned splendor" — a splendor imprisoned in the sense that we fail to realize and to release it. The Christ is not something apart and different from ourselves; He is the Real Self. Jesus so unified His psychological nature and His spiritual nature that

God spoke and acted through Him. He said, " *I do nothing of myself*"; *"The Father that dwelleth in me; he doeth the works."*

Look where you will in the New Testament, you will find the golden Truth running through every book that all men share the divine Spirit. When the people chose to worship the personality of Jesus instead of God, He said, *"It is expedient that I go away: for if I go not away, the Comforter will not come unto you.* [That is; You are mistaking a person for a Principle, but the Spirit will awake the Truth in you that I have been talking about]." The most that any teacher can do for us is to show us the divine possibilities that are latent in our souls. The uncovering and embodiment of these possibilities is up to us.

To practice the Presence, we must not only provide a psychological channel for the divine Guest to act through, but we must seek to "put on" (to personify) the Christ, as Jesus did. To Him, this Presence was very real. He talked to It as we would talk with another person. Do we talk with God? Yes, we do. Since we are all individualization of the One Life, there is no one else to talk to. We draw upon the divine Presence in such degree as we become aware of it.

This practice is not something mystical, complicated, and difficult; it is really very simple and easy. It assumes that within each man is an invisible Presence, that this Presence is God individualized in man, that there is no barrier between man and Him but belief, and that as much of this Reality as he releases through his awareness is spiritual Power.

One of the truly spiritual members of my congregation said to me recently, "I have moments when I Practice the Presence, but my greatest problem is to be conscious of the Presence of

God at all times." That is a common difficulty among Truth students. Many make the unfortunate mistake of trying to force God to be present by using will power. But God is Spirit, and Spirit is not under the dominion of the human will. Jesus made this clear when He said, *"Not my will, but thine, be done."* Until we bring the human will into subjection to the divine will, we shall never rise any higher than the physical world of sense.

We need to realize that God is already present and that there is no place in the universe from which He is ever absent. If you, like my friend, are ever troubled by a sense of God's absence, silence your doubts and cling to your intuitive knowledge. Remind yourself that you are a focus of that Life, Love, and Intelligence which is God and that you cannot be separated from your Source. Know that your only reason for existing is to express your Creator and that nothing can break the unity between the Creator and the Created. He cannot and does not change. The change — the realization that you seek — must take place in you. He will always be wherever you conceive Him to be.

God can be seen only with the inner eye. The man who follows God with his senses only sees nothing and hears nothing. He forgets that God is Spirit and that *"they who worship Him must worship Him in spirit and in truth."* The Voice does speak. The Light does shine. The mystic touch does come, not through the senses but through the spiritual faculties. They come when we accept the Presence and not before.

The first thing that Blind Bartimaeus did when Jesus sent for him was to *"cast away his garments"* so that nothing would stand in the way of his response. To Jesus' question, "What wilt thou that I should do unto thee?" the blind man answered, *"Lord, that I might receive my sight."* Not many of us realize the importance of being ready to receive the good things that *"God hath prepared for them that love Him."* If we are not receptive to the good God has prepared for us, it avails us nothing. We must get personality out of the way of the Divine Circuit for the particular good we seek to get through.

The Presence of God is always with us in the same way that the principle of mathematics is always with us. We put the principle of mathematics to work through recognition and acceptance. So it is with Principle. God becomes active in us through our recognition and our embodiment of the Presence.

His Life, Power, and Substance are ever ready to flow through us, our loved ones, and our affairs when we have unified our psychological natures and our spiritual natures to such a degree that the Christ is personified in us. Jesus himself said, *"Lo, I am with you always even unto the end of the world."* Then how can He be absent anywhere except in our belief?

Jesus said, *"Behold, I come quickly, and my reward is with me."* When we put God first in all things, the difficulties in our lives begin to straighten out. Our affairs fall into divine order; wholeness is established in our being. Like the blind man who *"immediately received his sight,"* we, too, immediately receive the fulfillment of our desire. Demonstration follows the acceptance of Truth, the realization of unity with God, the establishing of a foundation of faith.

The pattern is always the same: Believe and receive. If we do not receive the blessing we have asked for, we have failed in one of three ways:

1. We do not have the mental equivalent of the thing we are requesting.

2. The desire is not spiritually legal; that is, it is harmful to some one else.

3. Our ego is in the way.

When we comply with the three conditions, we become *"Such as hear the word and receive it,"* and we may expect our prayers to *"bring forth fruit some thirtyfold, some sixty, and some an hundred."*

When we practice the Presence of God, we bring our total life under the control and direction of divine wisdom. *"If any man be in Christ, he is a new creature: old things are passed away, behold, all things are become new."* Problems are solved. Harmony is restored. Desires are fulfilled. Obstacles are removed. Conditions are changed. Sickness disappears. All our affairs are brought into adjustment with Divine Law.

When we practice the Presence of God, we are controlled by a Power that knows only good, works only for good, and attracts only good. We are governed by an Intelligence that sees all things and does all things wisely. We are illumined by a Light that penetrates darkness of every kind and form. We are dominated by a Will that brings freedom, happiness, and joy. We are animated by a Love that brings harmony, healing, and peace.

Are you undecided as to what you should do? Are you uncertain as to which way you should go? Then take your problem into the Presence and ask Christ to tell you. Do not worry, strain, or fret about it. God knows which way you should go, and He will lead you. Place the whole matter lovingly in His hands, and let Him open the way for you. "But how shall I know that it is the right decision?" you ask. "Suppose that I make a mistake?" you say. And I answer, "When God is in charge of your life, and you listen to Him, you can depend upon the decisions which you make." Personal vision is limited. We see at best only a small part of the whole; Intelligence has no limitation of time or space and is not affected by the appearance of any situation or circumstance. It operates on the Law of Harmony. Having made a decision with His help, you must at once surrender any responsibility for working it out to Him and know forever afterward that the decision was right and good. Let no outward appearance shake your confidence. Say often to the Presence within, "I know that you are solving my problem now and I am grateful."

Are you distressed because you have lost something? Stop looking. Take the matter to God and ask Him to find it for you. The Scriptures tell us that *"there is nothing covered that shall not be revealed."* The thing to do is to affirm confidently, "Nothing is lost in Divine Mind," to surrender the missing article into God's hands, and to forget it. It will be found if you are faithful and accept this help, "nothing doubting."

But our difficulties and problems indicate our need for a greater consciousness of God's Presence. Many times the problems that harass and trouble us most can be met by a simple adjustment in consciousness. Instead of praying for deliverance from a particular difficulty, we should ask that the condition that is causing the discord be revealed to us in order that we may take the action that will correct it. That is what the Prodigal Son did when he came to himself. By re-directing his thoughts and facing his situation, he returned to his father's house. He was restored to the consciousness of wholeness, and all his needs were supplied.

When you take a difficult situation to God in the right spirit, one of two things happens: it is changed, or you find that you have the power and understanding to overcome it. Are there closed doors in your life? God can open them for you. Are you lost, confused, frustrated, and fearful? Remember that God knows the way. There is a Light within you that is greater than all the darkness in the world. That Light can bring you back into the path of freedom and peace. Do you face illness in yourself or in a loved one? *"The Sun of righteousness shall arise with healing in his wings."*

Few persons today have an absolute consciousness of Truth. Until the time arrives when that is established, we should use all the means of healing at our command. If one can meet sickness through his faith and understanding, he grows in the process and becomes stronger than before. But if such factors as the race thought, the emotional climate of the immediate environment and the evidence of the physical senses overwhelm him, he should recognize that the skill of the physician is also a form of expression of Intelligence and a means of hearing aid avail himself of it. God is the source of medical science as well as spiritual science. Many good doctors recognize this relationship and advise patients to send for their spiritual directors when they send for their doctors.

When we go to pieces and become panicky and fearful in the illness of a loved one, we hinder him instead of helping him. What he needs at such a time is the healing power of our constructive and loving thought. Instead of sending negative and destructive thoughts to tear him down, we must send positive and constructive thoughts to build him up. We must place him in the current of divine power by taking him into the Presence of God and leaving him there. We must see him as whole, strong, and well. We must look through the evidence of the physical senses to the spiritual perfection within.

There may be dark, fearful, and anxious moments, but every time we allow ourselves to worry, we take the patient out of God's Presence. Desire for the speedy healing of a loved one must be matched with an even greater willingness to leave him in God's hands and under the operation of His Will. Only under these conditions can the healing Power be set in motion. If we are troubled by the thought that God may want to take our loved one home, we must remind ourselves that God takes nothing from us but ills and illusions. The only way to keep our loved ones safe and secure is to daily hold them in the Presence.

Be perfectly natural in your approach to God. Ask Him for what you want, and then thank Him for the fulfillment of your desire. This will not only help to bring your loved one under the healing forces of Divine Mind and the operation of the Divine Will but will deepen your faith in God's loving and protective care.

Do you have obligations to meet and see no way of meeting them? Then face the situation in calmness and faith. Know that you are drawing upon the Kingdom of unlimited Good and that this Kingdom is here now — closer to you than the the breath of your own body. Place your need under the direction of divine Wisdom and know that God will meet it promptly and completely. Sing with the Psalmist, *"Heaven and earth are full of Thee."* There is plenty and to spare of everything; it is your Father's good pleasure to have you share this abundance.

Are you lonely? Do you find yourself overcome with a sense of separateness even in a crowd? Do you feel the lack of congenial companionship? Jesus was never alone and neither are you. You can develop the consciousness of the living Presence within you as He did. Then no longer will you think and speak of God *and* man; your concept will be man in God, God *over* all, in all, *through* all, *under* all; an indivisible God — whole in you and in every man; a God everywhere equally present at all times.

THE TECHNIQUE OF PRACTICE

There are five steps which will help you in developing the habit of Practicing the Presence.

1. Consciously work to form the concept of the Indwelling God.

2. Form a partnership with this Presence.

3. Recognize the unity of the spiritual and the physical.

4. Develop a dogged persistence in bringing your understanding into experience.

5. Eliminate the self by increasingly thinking of God.

1. Consciously work to form the concept of the Indwelling God.

The first step in Practicing the Presence of God is to form in your consciousness the idea that Christ is with you as a living, inherent, inseparable Power. Draw deeply upon your feeling and imagination until your awareness of His Presence becomes sure and strong. Be alert for instances in which the Law of Harmony (His law) is operating. Did you awake refreshed and ready for the day? Was your first hour one of anticipation and expectancy? Did you experience joy as you met with or worked with others through the day? Were meetings opportune? Did time lend itself to your needs and plans? Were you successful in what you did? Were you conscious of the Presence in others even for a moment? Did you catch a glimpse of a plan, a pattern, of which you were a part?

Learn to look for evidence of the God-Power within small things as well as great. Miracles do happen. Specific prayers are answered. But is there any greater happiness than that of harmonious living? He is where you look for Him; the Power is constantly operating.

Train yourself to be conscious of His Presence in moments of joy and ecstacy; in the meeting of minds; in shared laughter; in triumph and in victory; in your appreciation of the beautiful in music art and literature. See Him in times of distress, of grief, of discord, and of tribulation. Find Him in the mountains, the clouds, the breeze, the earth and its bounties. Recognize Him in the office, the store, the street, the classroom, the courtroom; in the home stricken by sorrow, in the sickroom, at the mortuary.

Express gratitude for your every recognition of His part in your clay. Take time for an unspoken "thank you," not only for the action but for your increasing ability to recognize the Presence and to identify yourself with It.

2. Form a partnership with God.

The housewife performing the many duties of the home, the salesman calling on his customers, the workman at his bench, the business man in his store, the clerk behind the counter, the driver of a car — each has a silent Partner. His hand is at the wheel, He walks beside us down the street, He rides with us on the bus. No matter where we are or what we may be doing, He is always With us. Converse with Him as you would with a friend. Tell Him about your problems, worries, and difficulties and tell Him that you need His help. Place your adversities and cares in His hands; accept the fact that He is working your problems out for you at that moment. When you run into a dead-end street, put the problem squarely up to Him and realize that He will show you a way you have not yet seen. Know that the Power you release has no limitation. The Christ Presence is Light and Life to everything it touches. Fulfill your obligation as a partner. Keep your conscious mind open and free from prejudice, jealousy, animosity. Recognize yourself as an instrument, a tool, a voice, a channel through which Good is expressing. Realize too that the privileges you have as a partner are shared by everyone else. Salute the spiritual man in everyone you meet. Recognize the vastness of the existing partnership as it operates in the One Mind and under the One Law, freed from the limitations of time and space.

3. Recognize the unity of the spiritual and the physical.

We tend to divide the world into two parts — the material and the spiritual. The belief in this partition must be broken down. There are only two factors to consider — the Creator and the created. To Practice the Presence successfully, we must see the universe as a whole. What can be the purpose of man (the created) except to embody and express his Creator? *"Glorify God in your body and in your spirit, which are God's,"* directed St. Paul. Contemplate for one moment the perfection of man's physical being, the intricate systems of circulation and digestion, the selectiveness of the senses, the pattern of the bones, muscles, sinews, the beauty and symmetry of the body. Stop long enough to review the order of the world he lives in . . . its movements, its place in the solar system, its minerals, vegetation, and animal life. Then you may get a momentary glimpse of the vision of the Creator. Think too of man s great gifts in his ability to think, to communicate through speech with others, to plan, to act individually and in cooperation, to make increasing use of the forces of nature, and to be aware of himself and his purpose. A divided universe? No. A divided man? Again, no. But a unified world and a whole man made possible by the Presence.

4. Develop a dogged persistence in bringing your under-standing into experience.

The world is full of people who have climbed to great heights in spite of the many obstacles and opposition in their paths. They have determined to go on in the face of disaster and disappointment, and their desires have been fulfilled. We can understand the result because the more we practice the Presence, the greater our power becomes. Success in spiritual work is a matter of persevering until victory and triumph have been achieved. When we are determined to succeed, the Power responds quickly and powerfully to our desire.

Recall stories of people who have lost everything and won it all back again simply because they would not admit failure and loss. They proved to themselves that one with God is a majority and that the Presence is always there waiting to be called forth.

There are outstanding illustrations of the fact that man-power plus God-Power is greater than any physical handicap, imperfection, disease, limitation, or weakness. Many persons who were given up by the doctors to die have refused to accept the dictum and have outlived their doctors. Success is a matter of making up our minds and holding on through thick or thin. When the wholeness of man is recognized, it can be realized. When Mind is called into action, the impossible becomes possible.

Are you in the grip of some destructive habit or abnormal appetite that is sapping your strength and ruining your health? Surrender it to the Presence and bring all the powers of your being into action against it. Know that the Presence is stronger and more powerful than any perverse and abnormal appetite and that He is producing the freedom which you desire. When habits are persistent, only greater persistence will overcome them. God takes full charge of a problem when it is fully placed in His Hands. Many. people have difficulty in surrendering a habit such as alcoholism because the physical desire for liquor is stronger than the spiritual desire for freedom. These persons have only partially made up their minds and will get only partial results. This should not discourage them, however; the steady dropping of water on a rock will gradually wear it away. The affirmative factor in breaking habit is not the number of failures but the persistence of the trend of thought. If we keep moving toward the perfect, any bondage will finally be broken.

5.   Eliminate the self by increasingly thinking of God.

We must eliminate the little self so that the Greater Self can be born. *"The natural man* [little self] *receiveth not the things of the Spirit of God: for they are foolishness unto him; neither can he know them."*

Someone has wisely said:

> "Anything of myself is too much.
> Talent stripped of self becomes genius;
> Courage stripped of self becomes heroism;
> Ability stripped of self becomes greatness;
> Humanity stripped of self becomes divinity."

The crying need of our age is not more gadgets, airplanes, and automobiles but the use of more time for Christ. That is why this fifth step in our technique is so important. Jesus' disciples spent twenty-four hours a day with Him for a period of three years. Is it any wonder that we have so little power to use and understand things spiritual when we give so little time to the Spirit?

The need cannot be met by setting aside a few moments a day for prayer, reading, and meditation. The solution lies in developing a twenty-four-hour awareness of His Presence.

Practicing the Presence is not a new project in spiritual endeavor. It has been known and practiced by the saints and spiritual giants of all ages. The stigmatists dwell upon the wounds in Jesus' Body until they reproduce the subcutaneous hemorrhages in their own hands and feet. The metaphysical student meditates upon the Christ Presence until It becomes real in his life.

There are many ways to meditate; each person must find the way that is most helpful to him.

One way of meditation is to concentrate upon such attributes of God as Life, Truth, Love, Justice, Wisdom, Knowledge, Understanding, Power, Peace, Beauty, Order, and to accept these qualities as our own. Visualizing them in action in our lives helps us to put them into practice; as we put them into practice, we are truly Practicing the Presence.

The Twenty-Third and Ninety-First Psalms are favorites of many, both as a means to achieve stillness and quiet and as the content of the meditation.

If words interest you, concentration upon the meaning of a specific word is helpful in setting up a train of thought that will lead to meditation. Take, for example, the word *establish*. How have you heard it used? People say, "That is an old established firm," "He established a home in San Francisco," "He established a name for himself by his work." What does the word mean? *Stable* is a part of it. What does *stable* mean? Perhaps these words will come to your mind: solid, enduring, fixed, permanent, steadfast, proved, accepted, settled, fixed, grounded.

How is the word used in the Bible? The concordance will lead you to such verses as these:

"And God said unto Noah, This is the token of the covenant, which I have established between me and all flesh that is upon the earth."

"But the Lord is faithful who shall establish you and keep you from evil."

"It is a good thing that the heart be established with grace."

"Be established in the present truth."

"Believe in God, so shall ye be established."

Then connect the word with your desire. Form your own declaration, weighing each word and live in it:

MY HEALTH (SUPPLY, FRIENDSHIPS, SUCCESS)
IS EVEN NOW ESTABLISHED IN GOD.

St. John said, *"No man hath seen God at any time"*; *"They that worship Him must worship Him in spirit and in truth."* This is the concept that we desire to build. There are many, however, who feel that concrete reminders of His Presence are helpful.

Many persons like to have statues or pictures of Jesus in their rooms or meditation chambers so that they will be reminded of the One who completely and wholly identified himself with God. Others carry small colored pictures of Jesus in their pockets or pocketbooks so that they are reminded of their privilege of Practicing the Presence every time they use them.

In some homes, there is a special chair for Him in the bedroom. Visualizing seems to make it easier for some persons to talk with Him about the activities, difficulties, and problems of the day, to pour out the heart to Him, to ask Him questions about the things that are troublesome, and to listen in the silence for the *"still small voice"* that is His. Some families keep a special chair at the table to remind members of the Unseen Guest during mealtimes.

A red-letter Bible in which the words spoken by Jesus are printed in ruby may provide a stimulus to your realization of the Presence. Pause after each sentence to ponder its meaning. Get the feeling that He is actually there speaking His words through you.

What we are really doing in this step is forming a new habit. The results may be slow at first, but thinking of God soon becomes automatic. In fact, we can come to the place eventually where we think God into the whole day. We can bring Him into every situation and condition in our lives by talking to Him about people we pass on the street, saying swift prayers for them as they look at us, holding such a thought for them as, "God lives in you and is now manifesting his perfect Being"; by thinking of Him as being in every group in which we happen to be; by calling His name when we go to answer the telephone with the thought—"One of God's children now wishes to speak to me."

Start this practice today and a wonderful new sense of power and exhilaration will develop within you. *"Whatsoever ye do} do all to the glory of God.*" Share your joy with Him. When you find yourself in an intolerable situation, think of God and He will be there by your side. Talk to Him about your work; ask for help on each difficult assignment and you will do a better job. When you have a letter to write, dedicate your hand and mind to God. Ask for Wisdom to flow through you, and you will write a much better letter. Pray for your customers while you are waiting on them. Bring God into your sales activities, bookkeeping, teaching, welding, carpentering, plumbing, typing, washing dishes, cleaning the house, doing the laundry, and you will always do the job better and with less strain.

If you, as a student, are fearful about an examination, ask God to give you a clear mind and a retentive memory. Ask Him to help you to know that He is Intelligence, Wisdom, and Knowledge and that you are one with Him. Pray before you go into a football or basketball game; what you ask for yourself, ask for every other member of the team — not that you may win the game but that you may play clean and fair and may make full use of your power. If you happen to be in a hospital, pray for all those who are waiting on you, doctors, nurses, internes, orderlies; see them as perfect instruments in His service. Pray for health and wholeness to be realized by all the other patients in the hospital even as you pray for yourself.

If you have difficulty in sleeping, tell Him about it and ask Him to meet this need for you. Recall the promise: *"He giveth his beloved sleep."* Then as you lie down on your pillow, feel his fingers gently touching his eyelid, sealing them in a deep and restful sleep. Feel His Presence slowing down and dissolving all the tension in your body. When you turn off your light, know that *"He that keepeth Israel neither slumbers nor sleeps."*

If you are having trouble in solving a particularly difficult problem, go into the Silence before you go to sleep and say over and over again to yourself: "I contact within me the Christ Presence of Wisdom, Power, and Guidance." Say this and feel the truth of the statement until you are convinced that the contact has been made. Then talk to the Presence about your problem and tell Him of your desire in connection with it. Try to realize that He is at that moment solving the problem for you. Know forever afterward that you have turned it over to a greater power than your own. Say each time the problem returns to your thought, "Father, I thank. Thee that Thou art solving this problem for me now." If fear creeps into the picture, meet it with such statements as these: "God's activity for me is instant, complete, and sustained", or "The Christ Presence in me is an irresistible Power creating my good for me instantly."

PRAYER FOR THE PRESENCE

God, I recognize your Presence in me, "closer than breathing and nearer than hands or feet." I know that you are the Reality and Truth of me. With all my heart, I desire to express only this Reality and this Truth. I know that you are equally present in others, and I ask help to see through the unreality of appearance to the Christ within each man. I am grateful for the Good which I have been able to accept. I pray that I may daily grow in power to accept and demonstrate more and more Good.

I accept the privilege of your companionship with joy and thanksgiving. I consciously clear every avenue of impression so that I may become increasingly aware of your Presence. I open wide all the channels of expression in order that You may speak and act through me.

I approach the coming night and the new day confidently, for I know that your Presence will sustain me, guide me, bless me. I know that I am where I am now because I am in my right place. I know that there is no problem to meet, no joy to experience, no grief to bear, no success to face in which I will be alone.

Chapter X
Magnifying the Light

This is an age of light. Electric light, violet light, neon light, black light, X-rays, Beta rays and light in countless other forms serve man. But there is another Light that transcends in power every form of material light. It is the beneficent and protecting power of the luminous energy flowing directly from God that illumines the lives of those who accept the promise, *"Christ shall give thee light,"* and fulfill their responsibility.

"Ye are the light of the world," said Jesus. The mystical Light is in you; it is at the very center of your being now. It is the same light that led Moses and his people through the wilderness, that blinded St. Paul on the highway to Damascus. Stop right now and think of the cries and emergencies in your life. Have there not been time when you were on the brink of disaster when you came shockingly near to the edge of the precipice but did not fall over? Have there not been times when every door was closed to you, but you go out? Have there not been times when you almost died but didn't? If you are honest to yourself, you will have to admit that these escapes were not purely accidental.

"But this is all so mystical," you say. That is true; all the followers of Christ are mystics. They are mystics in the sense that they are endeavoring to shape their lives by the mystical and unseen forces of Spirit. The mystic sees the Light; and while he cannot explain what he sees, it brings all good into his life. Acknowledging One Presence and One Power, he is able to look beyond the impoverished, weak, and diseased conditions of the lower realm and behold the pulsating vigor and glowing health of the radiant Christ who *"forgiveth all our iniquities and healeth all our diseases."* Into the life of every seeker after Light comes this flash of illumination from the Source of Light. Behold the dazzling light around Jesus when He came down from the Mount of Transfiguration! This same Light brought Admiral Byrd back to civilization from his ice cave in the Antarctic and kept Eddie Rickenbacker and his men alive in the little rubber craft adrift on the sea. It is the Light that opens prison doors, unlocks mysteries, provides intuition, clarifies problems — the Light that protects man in danger, guides him into the right way, delivers him from bondage, and meets his every emergency.

Just as carrion exposed to the sun is quickly dissolved by the purifying and penetrating power of the rays, the darkness of human thinking is dispelled by the Light of Truth.

God brought order out of chaos with the creative phrase, *"Let there be light."* All through the Bible, the Light is recorded as lighting the ways of man. The Psalmist cries out, *"Lord, lift Thou up the light of Thy countenance upon us,"* and again, *"Thy word is a lamp unto my feet, and light unto my path."* There is a thundering admonition in the Sermon on the Mount: *"Ye are the light of the world. A city that is set on a hill cannot be hid. Neither do men light a candle, and put it under a bushel but on a candlestick; and it giveth light to all that are in the house."* And there is the command, *"Let your light so shine before men that they may see your good works, and glorify yow · Father which is in Heaven."*

Light is one of the great mysteries of life. No one knows what it is any more than he knows what electricity is. Analyzing certain of its characteristics may help our understanding of the Light.

Light is always pure. It cannot be soiled or contaminated in any way. Water flowing down a dirty street becomes impregnated with the dirt through which it flows. Light, on the other hand, is not changed by the conditions through which it shines. Light shining through a dirty window pane does not become soiled. When we were children looking at the light through colored glass, it seemed as though we had changed the light, but we hadn't. The light itself was untouched; the glass limited the amount of light that got through.

Light can be reflected. It is reflected on the physical plane by mirrors or other shining surfaces; we reflect light by thinking spiritually and by living so that the Light is manifest to all. Others cannot live by our Light, but they can see and recognize its effect on our lives.

The Light is not something that we hand from one to another as we would an electric light globe; we give it to others by being the Light ourselves. Illumination, like Cosmic Consciousness, is a gift vouchsafed to very few, but the few have proved it a Reality. They have seen a Presence — a luminous substance penetrating and inter-penetrating everything. They have seen the truth of the Psalmist's statement: *"Heaven and earth are full of Thee."* The very air that we breathe is charged with this luminous substance that cleanses as it floods all the dark places in body and in mind. The aura around the human body is not the phenomenon of psychic science but the emanation of that Light *"that lighteth every man that cometh into the world."*

Light is the same wherever we find it. If we follow artificial light to its source, we see that it is only transmuted light. Where does it come from? From the generators at the light plant. Where do the generators get their power? From coal. What is coal? Coal is plant life that stored up light energy millions of years ago. So you see there is really no artificial light. It is only the name we give to the way man has made use of one form of it. We find the Light in unexpected places and sometimes fail to recognize It for what It is. Someone voices his righteous conviction in the face of opposition, a little child speaks, a stranger smiles, unfaltering trust persists through poverty and affliction, a specific problem in our lives is solved—and this is Light.

The use of the word, *Light,* as a synonym for God is a means of enlarging our spiritual understanding. Throughout the Bible, the word is used figuratively, over and over.

Light is a symbol of life. *"In him was life, and the life was the light of men."* Light and life have the same meaning. Where God is, there is light; where light is, there is life. Does not the doctor tell us that the best way to destroy disease, filth, and germs is to expose the dark places to the light? Light is life-giving; darkness is death-dealing. Just as termites multiply in the dark and secluded places of a building, disease breeds in the dark places of the mind.

Light is a symbol of the spiritual or uplifted consciousness. The *"children of light"* referred to in the Bible are those who have surrendered personal consciousness for Christ Consciousness. Christ Consciousness represents Spirit in action: *"He that followeth me shall not walk in darkness, but shall have the light of life."* The New Testament is very clear on the subject. If one dwells in spiritual consciousness (walks with the Indwelling Presence), he is secure. If he does not, he is in outer darkness.

Light is a symbol of one-pointedness. Dr. James Moffatt says, "To walk in or by the light is to have one's character and conduct determined by the influence of Christ, the latter being as indispensable to vitality in the moral and religious sphere as light is to physical growth."

Jesus said, *"The light of the body is the eye: if therefore thine eye be single, thy whole body shall be full of light. But if thine eye be evil* [double], *thy whole body shall be full of darkness."* Let us think about these words.

The *"light"* is the Light of which Jesus spoke when He said, *"I am the Light of the World."* It is the light of Truth; it is the Principle by which all spiritual demonstrations are made.

The *"body"* referred to does not mean the physical organism alone, but the entire life — body, mind, and spirit. It is the total of man's affairs — home, family, business, job, concerns.

The *"eye"* is the upper eye of the mind — that visional faculty by which we see into the other world which Jesus described as The Kingdom of Heaven. It is that capacity by which we see through appearances to Reality. If the lower eyes are closed and the upper eyes are opened (*"single"* as Jesus said), the *"body"* is harmonious.

Why was Jesus able to open blind eyes, unstop deaf ears, and heal all manner of disease? Because His attention was focused on a Higher Plane than that in which we habitually function. Looking beyond the three-dimensional world of false beliefs in two realities, He did not see disease, weakness, and evil; He saw the perfect life of all creation. Seeing Reality in every situation, He called it forth.

There is an old saying which runs something like this: "There are two pairs of eyes in man. It is necessary that the pair beneath should be closed when the pair above them perceive;

and when the pair above are closed, those which are beneath are opened." The thought in this statement appears often in the things that Jesus said and did. One of these is recorded in John 4:35: *"Say not ye, there are yet four months, and then cometh the harvest? behold, I say unto you, Lift up your eyes* [close the lower eyes and open the upper eyes] *and look on the fields; for they are white already to harvest.* [Look with the visional faculty, the single eye of Spirit, and see into a timeless realm where seed time and harvest are one.]"

On another occasion, He told the woman of Samaria at the well all the things she had ever done. He was able to do this because He was functioning in a consciousness in which the past, present, and future are one. Jesus did not see the leprosy, blind eyes, withered hands, and palsy of those who came to Him for healing. Seeing with the upper eyes of Spirit, He looked on wholeness, and it materialized with His recognition.

Healing is not a matter of repeating decrees and affirmations. It is not changing one physical condition for another. It is seeing the Truth. When the Higher Potential flows into the lower, the action and quickening are always the result of uplifted consciousness.

"Having eyes, see ye not? and having ears, hear ye not?" One of the most difficult things for a teacher of metaphysical science to do is to help people learn how to see and hear beyond the range of sensuous apprehension, how to close the lower eyes and open the upper eyes, how to focus the eyes on the plane of the eternally perfect. The ability comes with understanding, with practice, with growth.

All such problems as disease, bottlenecks, confusion, discouragement, empty pocketbooks, and weakness belong to the lower plane and result from imperfect vision. We correct and solve them by opening the eyes of spiritual perception and seeing the Truth.

Light is the symbol of a magnet. A magnet draws steel filings, but it will not draw wood or stones. In other words, it draws only those things for which it has an affinity. So it is with the Light. We are drawn to the source of Light because there is something divine in us which responds to the Light. If we were not akin to the Light, we could not be drawn to it.

The one who has accepted his responsibility as the Light of the World draws good toward him automatically. He draws others to him by reason of his radiance, his happiness, and his sense of well-being. His very appearance seems to say, *"Rejoice with me."* If we are not happy, we are not exercising our right as the *"children of God"*; we have indisputable evidence that we are not pleasing God and that we are not as spiritual as we wish to be.

What is there about a spiritual person that distinguishes him from one who is not spiritual? Is the question as baffling as an Iowa judge found the decision he had to make in a contested will case? A large sum of money — $75,000 — was left by a church member to persons who were Christians. The will was contested by members of the family who stated that since there is no common acceptance of what constitutes the Christian religion, no one really knows what a Christian is.

What do we, in the metaphysical field, mean when we say that a person is spiritual? How do we arrive at such a conclusion? On what basis do we make such an assertion? And why do we impute spirituality to one person and not to another? Is it something that we see in the person, or is it something we feel, or is it both? It is both. But to understand this matter, we must turn for our authority to the First Epistle of John, the fourth to seventh verses.

"This then is the message which we have heard of Him, and declare unto you, that God is light, and in Him is. no darkness at all.

If we say that we have fellowship with Him, and walk in darkness, we lie, and do not the truth: But if we walk in the light, as He is in the light, we have fellowship one with another, and the blood [spirit, life] *of Jesus Christ, his son, cleanseth us from all sin."*

The spiritual man, then, is distinguished from other men by a certain light that shines through him. *"If we walk in the light,"* *"we have fellowship with Him."* We are spiritually His sons. The distinguishing mark of a spiritual person is the evidence of the illumination of his consciousness. He is the one who brings insight, power, perception, and understanding into every circumstance, situation, and incident.

A little girl going through a cathedral asked her mother who the people were in the stained glass windows. She was told they were the saints. Then one morning at Sunday School class when the teacher was talking about St. Paul, St. John, St. Peter, she put up her hand and said, "I know who the saints are. They are the Christians who let the light shine through."

Here is the answer to our question: A spiritual person is he who lets the Light shine through. Illumined by the radiant energy of spirit, he brings light to every subject.

St. Paul referred to *"the rulers of the darkness of this world."* The same darkness works today through alcohol, dope, drugs, gluttony, and sensual excesses. The results of these forces are graphically set forth in government reports of many kinds. The daily newspapers provide evidence that men who are under the influence of liquor and dope are open to the force of darkness and easily controlled by them. Crime, confusion, discord, dissension, and sickness bear witness to the need for Light.

Probably someone at this point will want to argue the statement: *"God is light and in Him is no darkness at all."* But just a minute! You and I are like the soldier at the front seeing only one segment of the picture and trying to figure out the plan of the battle. We are like the fly on the steeple that says, "My! What a big world !" When we look at conditions in the world, we see only a small part of the picture. The world, like a coin, has two sides, and it is impossible for us now to see both sides at once. God has a plan for this world, and that plan is succeeding whether we recognize it or not. When we are able to raise our consciousness high enough, we shall see the world as it is and not as it appears to be. We shall view it with understanding and sympathy. It is enough for us to know now that, since the Reality of man is Spirit, the important thing is not what happens to the body but what happens to the soul.

Are you letting the light from your own Indwelling Christ shine, or are you still walking in darkness? Where are you today? How far have you come toward the Light? Do you carry critical, negative, and pessimistic attitudes? Are you overwhelmed by the things that happen to you? Then you are still in the darkness. The Light for some reason cannot get through.

How are you preventing the Light from shining in your life? Is it there but burning low? Then put in a larger bulb. Increase your wattage. St. Luke said, *"Let your loins be girded about, and your lights burning."* That is a wonderful text for anyone whose light is lowered. There is a sense of expectancy in it. There is activity in it. There is a great feeling of power and accomplishment about it. What picture does it bring to your mind? I see a track man, with rippling muscles playing in the sun. The light plays upon his lithe and eager form. His whole body is tense with anticipation; his eyes glisten with victory as he listens for the starter's "On your mark. Get ready. Get set! Go!"

Man often blunders because he follows the faint and flickering light of his own poor wisdom or accepts the reflected and uncertain light of others. Borrowed light is like that of the moon which has no light of its own and shines only when the sun's rays fall upon it. If you live by borrowed light, you are probably de pending upon the personality of another. This kind of dependency arrests your growth and dims your comprehension. Man often profits by the experience of another, but in this area each must find the Light for himself. God is to any individual whatever he conceives Him to be. He responds on the plane on which He is met. How then can you claim another's understanding as your own? How can you know yourself as you are in God? How can you pray without doubt? How can you enter into the consciousness of the Presence?

Start with the Light you already have — the Light *"which lighteth every man that cometh into the world"* — the Light you were born with. Free that Light! Let It shine! Open the casement windows. Abolish the curtains and shutters. Fling wide the door. Tear down the vines around the porch. When you look to the Source of Light, you find a great change coming about in your life and affairs. You feel more alive than ever before. Commonplace things are glorified. Difficult tasks become easy. Everything in your world is transformed for the better. The Light of God is to your soul what the rays of the sun are to the germ in the planted bulb. It is the life of your being.

One of the amazing things about living in the Light is that we are so often guided into the things we have subconsciously wanted to do all our lives. Here is a story that illustrates this point.

A widow, who had walked many a long mile on shoes whose soles were daily reinforced with paper to make them last longer, came at last to the end of her rope. She returned one night to her room to find it rented to another and her few posessions held back for rent. Seeking shelter for the night in a basement entrance, she prayed as she had never prayed before. She was directed to look up an old friend whom she had not even thought of for years. With open arms her friend received her. "Oh, Addie," she cried. "If I was ever glad to see a body, I am glad to see you. Will you stay with me a while and help me make some school clothes for my children?"

Back through the years the hungry woman's mind darted to the time when even as a young girl her heart's desire had been to make clothes for children. She went at the work offered her with real joy and enthusiasm, and the wardrobe she turned out for the children of her friend was the envy of the neighborhood. A salesman for a house dealing in children's wearing apparel noticed the clever designs and asked the woman if she would care to submit some of them to his shop. That was the beginning of a fine business for her. The light of God was with the woman, even as it is with you. It directed her in doing a work that had always seemed like play to her.*

---

* Used by permission of Weekly Unity.

Are you falling in the business of living? Then step into this Light and It will send you forth with new life, new faith, new hope, new affections, and new ideas. Lose yourself in the Light, and It will light away all the false desires, abnormal appetites, and bad habits that have been holding you in bondage. Make it the great absorbing desire of your life, and It will lead you into that happiness, fullness, and completeness of Life that God has ordained for you from the beginning. All you have to do is to recognize It, live by It, and be It. "But I have so many kinds of problems," you say. There is only one problem — the darkness of the human mind. Dissolve this darkness, and everything else falls into its right place. Even as Jesus went to. Bethany to awaken Lazarus out of sleep, so will Christ enter your consciousness to awaken you out of the darkness which is upon you.

When we turn on the light in a dark room, the darkness disappears. Where does it go? It doesn't go anywhere — it is dissolved and reduced to its native nothingness. When the Light of Truth is brought to bear upon any problem, however serious or confusing, the darkness that is in it ceases to exist, for the problem is solved by spiritual enlightenment.

Is your light burning low because you feel your prayers are not answered? They may be unanswered, but they are not lost. Praying is good if for no other reason than that failure or delay may cause you to examine your prayer to see whether it is spiritually legal, whether you really want what you are asking for and are willing to accept any responsibility that it might bring, and whether you are ready to give up what you are asking to have replaced.

But often you feel that your prayer has fallen on deaf ears when the answer is merely delayed. The calendar and the clock are man-made—made, of course, in accordance with the fixed movements of the earth but still man-made. So too is the table of linear measure. What may seem to you as delay may be only the wait for the right time.

Have you ever analyzed your experiences and discovered how many of the prayers you have forgotten about have been answered? Perhaps you did not recognize the answers when they came, but you took them for granted. The loved one for whose recovery you once prayed is now enjoying perfect health. The home you asked for is now in your possession. The job you wanted so desperately is now yours. Go back far enough in your experience, and you will be amazed at the number of answers did not come as you expected they would, but they came nevertheless.

Few persons fail to recognize that there is a Power greater than man although they call I by many different names. This awareness is the evidence of the Inherent Light. Man's task is to magnify It. How, then, do we magnify the Light? By consciously recognizing It. The soul receives direct Light from God, and we amplify It by removing all obstructions in the form of negative beliefs and dark thoughts. These tend to dim It until It becomes a mere flicker. When we identify ourselves with the Light, our prayers flash forth like lightning and open the way for us. Demonstrations, demonstrations, demonstrations follow—so many we cannot count them. With such speed does the Light operate in our affairs that we are astounded. We experience the Kingdom of Heaven here and now.

But the awareness of the Light places us under obligation, too. It is easier to sleep in the physical darkness than in the light. Sometimes we find it easier to ignore the Truth we sense and continue to sleep on. But *"Awake thou that sleepest, and arise from the dead and Christ shall give thee light"* is the command and the promise. Let us think through this verse together. What does it mean?

"Awake thou that sleepest." The sleepers are those who do not see beyond the senses, those who have not unified the outer self with the inner spiritual self.

"And arise from the dead." The *"dead"* are those who have accepted the mortal man as the real self — the self which St. Paul said is *"dead in trespasses and sins."* Trying to serve the mind of the flesh, they have cut themselves off from the Mind of God. This self must be put off so that the Real Self — the Christ Self — may take its place.

"And Christ shall give thee light." The Light is the Light indwelling every man. It is the Light of peace, power, and plenty. It is the light of health and wholeness. Light is the spiritual synonym for the wonderful manifestation of the riches and glory of the kingdom of Heaven. The Christ Self is always perfect and always One with the Father; for *"That which is born of the flesh is flesh; and hat which is born of the Spirit is Spirit."*

"Awake thou that sleepest, and arise from the dead, and Christ shall give thee light." Awake and turn your ailing body to the Light. Turn your darkened mind to the brightness of His glory. Seek not the perishable things of earth, but seek the Light. Instead of trying to demonstrate material things, turn on the Light. Let It shine through your disposition, attitudes, judgments,

and actions. The good things you desire will be manifested in your experience in proportion to the transparency and clarity of the medium the Light passes through.

"Ye are the Light of the world," said Jesus. What a wonderful statement that is! We are to lighten all the dark places of our world. We are to make clear the way of the Lord. We are to let our light shine in all directions. We are to lighten the burdens of others. We are to bring into every situation the transforming power and understanding of anew and illuminated mind. More than that, we are to see beyond the plane of weak, limited, sickly, and diseased conditions to the plane of Reality and Perfection. If you have to laid hold even in a small measure of the Great Light, Jesus' call is to you. *"Let your lights so shine before men."* Let it radiate to all those who blunder in darkness. Arm yourself with the weapons of faith and prayer against the dark forces that beset humanity. Expose the poison pockets of doubt, fear, greed, selfishness, prejudice, and other works of evil to the Light.

The Master Light is here, shining unto all the world. It is in you. It is your hope of glory. Align yourself with the spiritual forces of Light so that you may free yourself from every bond of ignorance, sickness, folly, and misunderstanding. Sing with the Psalmist, *"O send out thy light and thy truth: let them lead me; let them bring me unto thy holy hill."*

TECHNIQUE OF MAGNIFYING THE LIGHT

Jesus proved himself to be the truest, clearest medium for the Light that world has ever known. He was so perfect an agent that He became the Light and was enabled to say, *"I am the Light of the world."* In all ages there have been persons so aware of their unity with God, so sensitized to His Presence, so selfless, and so strong in faith that they were able to establish instantaneous communication with their Source and to manifest it for all the world to see. They were and are the blest. If you have this power, cherish it. You have no need of aids or devices.

But there are those of us who are so accustomed to thinking of the formality and discipline of our approach to what we desire and what we recognize as good that we do not have the full realization of our birthright. "We are reluctant to trust our intuition and feel that only by work and effort can we attain the end we seek.

The drill that follows is for the purpose of magnifying our inherent Light until we become conscious of our oneness with the Great Light. Through it, we may find the way by which we can best establish the contact we seek. We may find that we lengthen one step and shorten another as we become familiar with the procedure. We may find that we omit some of the suggestions. There is no ritual by which one needs to be bound. The practice that brings results is the right procedure, and each must determine that for himself.

Mystics of all time have developed and utilized practices that relax the body and eliminate psychic tension. The process is two-fold. Complete relaxation involves both the body and the mind.

Psychic tension is a psychological term which refers to such negative and distinctive mental and emotional states as worry, anxiety, fear, jealousy, resentment, and animosity. Psychic tension is like a tourniquet limiting the energy by which we are kept alive. Those who learn to overcome it prolong their lives on this plane many years. When the mind is relaxed, the body is at rest and man becomes a conductor through which the Light shines.

The first step in magnifying the Light is to relax the body. There are many postures which assist in this relaxation. One is sitting in a chair with the back straight and the arms resting lightly on the thighs with the palms of the hands turned upward. The other is lying flat on a hard bed or other surface with the arms resting loosely by the sides of the body and the feet about six inches apart. Each person must find the position in which he is most comfortable.

The second step is to think of the body as weighing a thousand pounds or more and being upheld by the surface on which it rests. You have no responsibility for this support except to surrender your body to it.

Now flex the muscles of your body from your feet to your neck. Squeeze every muscle as tightly as you can, just as though you were wringing water out of a bath towel. Let go as though you were coming unglued and your body were falling apart. Take a deep breath between flexings and exhale slowly without effort right down to your boots. Make sure that the lungs are emptied completely.

Now roll your head from side to side, touching your face to the bed each time as though it were not attached to your body. Inhale and exhale again, and turn your attention to the muscles of the face. Relax these muscles by drawing them up into a knot and then letting them go. Say to yourself, "My face is relaxed in perfect ease." Inhale and exhale again, and turn your thought specifically to your eyes. Squeeze the eyelids as tightly as you can and let the eyes open. Do this seven times. (*Seven* is the cardinal number symbolizing perfection and wholeness.) Say each time you flex the eye balls, "My eyes are the perfect eyes of Spirit and God sees now through them."

Repeat this practice with specific attention to the throat, tongue, neck, shoulders, arms, hands, lungs, abdomen, thighs, legs, knees, feet. Think of the Christ Presence as coming more and more into focus as you relax the physical body. Feel peace and serenity flowing through every nerve, muscle, tissue, and organ until you are no longer conscious of your body — until it makes no more claims upon you. Repeat many times, "The Healing Peace is now flowing through my body, relaxing, renewing, vitalizing, and healing it, making me perfectly whole, well, and complete." Remain quiet for a moment.

The next step is to relax the mind. What we are seeking in this exercise is relaxation of the total man — body and mind.

Now hold your body in a relaxed state and think of your mind — the whole mental realm — as an untroubled pool. Surrender your human will to the Divine Will. Repeat Jesus' own words: *"Not my will, but thine, be done."* Keep repeating them until the human will is no longer active in you. Now withdraw your mind from all concern with the outer world. Say to yourself, *"He will keep him* [me] *in perfect peace whose mind is stayed on Thee."* Withdraw your attention from your problems. Refuse for the moment to have any concern or thought about them. Repeat words and statements such as these to yourself:

Quiet- serenity- peace- poise- tranquility

"So long Thy Power has kept me,
Sure It still will lead me on."

"Where He leads me, I will follow;
I'll go with Him all the way."

Now "Let go and let God." Keep saying to yourself, *"I and the Father are one"* until you feel the peace and stillness of Spirit within you. Breathe such words as these: "I am enfolded by His Presence." "I am resting in the Secret Place of the Most High." "I am abiding under the Shadow of the Almighty."

The next step is to enter the Silence of the soul to contact God's Presence. You have shut the door of the senses and silenced all vagrant thoughts and are now at the door which takes you into God's Presence. *"Be still and know that I am God."* Say these words over several times quietly and with deep feeling. Say them until you feel the stillness in every atom of your being. The purpose of this step is to help you feel the Presence within you and unify yourself with God. *"Be still and know that I am God."* Know the Truth in these words. Feel it. You are approaching the Presence of God who is "closer . . . than breathing and nearer than hands and feet."

Now stretch your arms out to your sides and see yourself on the bed as surrounded with an aura or circle of light. Think of this Light as a radiation of the Great Light with which you are making contact. You have three physical inlets for making this contact—the top of your head, the soles of your feet, and the tips of your fingers. Think of all three as resting against the circle of Light which surrounds you.

Breathe the Light deeply into your being. Feel It penetrating every recess of your mind and every part of your body. *"In Him was life and the life was the light of men."*

Now as you inhale, visualize the light pouring through the top of your head, the soles of your feet, and the tips of your fingers. Your physical breathing goes on automatically; do not confuse it with the inbreathing of your Light Body.

Now visualize the aura of Infinite Light that comes direct from God as pouring through your being and centering in the soul. The soul is not located in the body but around the body. You can think of the point of concentration, however, as in the region of the solar plexus, the center of your abdomen just below the ribs. It is at this point that your light fuses with the Divine Light.

The next step is to *"put on the armor of light"*; do this by following round the aura of light in your thought.

As you consciously inhale the Light, turn your attention to the point just above your head and say silently or aloud, *"I am the Light of the world."* Visualize this light descending from the auric circle and entering your body through the solar plexus. Be very still during these exercises and feel the light of Spirit flowing through you, permeating your entire being. See yourself immersed in a sea of effulgent light illuminating your whole body. Now turn your thought toward the soles of your feet and repeat the process, saying *"I am the Light of the world."* Do the same thing with the tips of your fingers.

Your mind and body are now charged with light and your whole being is filled with peace. God is there, and you are ready to feel His Presence. You must be careful, however, not to try to visualize His Presence. Simply recall all the things you know about God and say, as Jesus did, *"I and the Father are one."* Then repeat the 23rd Psalm or any of the Scriptures that give you a vivid awareness of His reality and nearness. Your consciousness will be lifted to the point at which you can actually feel the Divine Presence.

The last step is to embody the Presence within your own consciousness. You must not only hope that this will happen;

you must also expect it to happen. Expectation is faith in action. Know that God will come into your consciousness at this point—not as a tangible form but as a state of mind. This is the reward for your effort. The moment you sense the Presence of God, that moment your desire has been fulfilled. You are now able to say your prayers and give your treatments with absolute certainty of an answer. You are aglow with divine possibilities; your mind is open to the influx of spiritual ideas; your world is filled with Light. "The Light that lighteth every man" is now aflame in you. Thank God before closing your meditation for the Light which He has bestowed upon you and all mankind.

To understand the thrill and wonders of the Light you must experience It. This is a very simple technique which anyone can practice. When we become the Light, we can share it with others. The problems in our lives and those of our loved ones are no longer our responsibility but His. Praying in the Light is providing a channel through which our desire is conducted to God and through which His power comes to meet our need.

Chapter XI
Releasing the Real Self

Do not be misled by the brevity of this chapter. These pages develop a concept presented in the chapter on healing . . . a concept that will change your life the instant that you grasp it—a concept that will bring into being the *"new man"* which you have long hoped to *"put on"*—a concept that will reveal to you a new heaven and a new earth.

Much of the content is in terms of physical healing, for that is the area in which most of us make our first explorations in search of well-being. But all that is said about healing applies equally to man's desire for other aspects of the good life. Inherently we want good and not evil; we want abundance and not lack; we want strength and not weakness; we want joy and not sorrow; we want security and not fear.

Are you seeking health? You will not find it in your body, for it has never been there. Health is an activity of the soul which is manifested in the body.

Sickness stems from the belief in a material body and the belief that we exist in this body; the belief that the functions of the body can be afflicted, corroded, clogged, diseased, disturbed, disorganized, and broken down; the belief that there are germs, bacteria, and virus that can infect, injure, poison, and destroy life.

Are you afraid of what may happen to your body? Then you need to change your relation to it.

If you believe that your life began when you entered your body, you also believe that your body can be crippled, emaciated, and diseased, and that your life can die.

But if we were living inside our bodies and bound by the ills and sufferings that flesh is subject to, our efforts at healing would be hopeless and futile. It is because we are living outside our bodies that they can be healed.

But there is something vastly more important than this. If we were living inside these physical bodies, as the materialists would have us believe, we should die when the body died. Our hope of immortality could not be fulfilled.

Do you believe that you have a life of your own? If you do, then again you limit your life. Jesus said, *"Whosoever liveth and believeth in me shall never die."* Do you see how this changes the picture? Whoever enters into and shares His quality of life or consciousness shall never come to the end of life, shall never experience the decomposition of life, regardless of what happens to the physical body. If we have the Life of God, our continuity is assured.

We heal disease by the understanding that the body is in Life, rather than by the belief that Life is in the body. The lesser is always in the greater.

"There is a natural body [which in a divided consciousness belongs to the lower or material plane and is subject to its destructions and limitations] *and there is a spiritual body* [which in a united consciousness belongs to the Higher or Spiritual plane and is not subject to disease, disintegration, or death]."

This Spiritual Body is Life itself. It bears no relation to time or space or individuality except as we impress these factors

146

upon It. How important it is then that we are selective in what we impress, for we determine in this way the conditions that materialize in our lives upon this plane. The Truth of Being is not bound except by our thought. Its scope is limited only by the degree of our understanding.

To be conscious of the Truth of Being, one must be absent from a material sense of body. Many people will no doubt be healed as they study this chapter, but they will be the people who have made this Truth an active part of their consciousness.

When St. Paul told us to *"Be absent from the body,"* he meant that we were to lose the material or physical sense of the body. What happens when we do this? We are *"present with the Lord."* Having separated ourselves from the false concept of the body, we find ourselves in the spiritual body.

Many people believe that they lose the body in death. This is an erroneous concept, for the body is a form of consciousness, and consciousness and its form can never be separated. The truth is that you and your real body can never be separated. In this world and the next they will always be together.

When you lose the material sense of the body, you also lose its ailments, aches, and pains. You are no longer concerned about it or any of its functions. In fact, you will have no more fear about it nor what may happen to it. You are beginning to experience the freedom that Jesus referred to when He said, *"Take no thought for the body."*

St. James said, *"Many are sick and weakly among you, not discerning the Lord's Body* [not having the spiritual sense of life]." These words obviously imply that the spiritual sense of life is essential to health and strength.

Jesus said, *"He that loseth his life shall find it.* [When we lose our material sense of life, we find the spiritual life.]"

Healing is accomplished not by exchanging one body for another body but by allowing the spiritual body to take its rightful place. When we understand that the body is a form of consciousness and not a material entity, we shall see that there is nothing to heal. The metaphysician does not try to change an unchangeable God but to change man's concept of Him in order to bring the objects of his desires within the realm of demonstration. The belief in a material universe is the cause of all our problems and ills; we solve the problems and cure the ills by changing our belief.

The spiritual healer does not change one bodily condition for another; he changes one state of consciousness for another. He changes the patient's belief about himself from a material to a spiritual basis.

The patient who believed that he was a physical-material body sees that he is a Spiritual Being, and his changed belief is objectified in his body and in his affairs. This is a basic truth in metaphysical practice. To be healed spiritually, we must have the consciousness of the Presence and Power of Spirit. If we do not have the realization of the Presence and Power of Spirit, the healing Principle does not work for us. We know from what has already been said that the Christ Presence is always with us, but it takes our consciousness of the Presence to do the healing.

The reason some systems do not succeed in spiritual healing is that they direct the attention to the physical body and try to do something about it. Spiritual healing on the other hand succeeds when the patient realizes that he is not in or of the physical body but is Spirit, or Christ Consciousness.

In spiritual healing, we take the position that God is the only Presence and Power in the Universe — the one and perfect Life of all Being — and we hold that position against all comers, against every appearance, belief, or suggestion that seems to deny it. We face any and every form of evil with Jesus' words: *"Thou couldest have no power at all against me, except it were given thee from above. [And this power has never been given to evil.]"* Evil in any form has no power except that which man gives it — eyes to see with, ears to hear with, lips to speak with and a body to act with.

There are many valuable things in this book but the thought in the preceding sentence is one of the most valuable. The only way we can heal or be healed is to change our belief about the condition that is troubling us. When we come to see that there is no reality, no power, no force, and no substance to maintain or sustain disease, we can heal ourselves and others of whatever needs to be healed.

We can do that just as soon as we see that all disease is an illusion. Since Christ, the healer, the patient and the belief are all in consciousness, the healing and correction must take place there. So we, as healers, treat ourselves for what the patient believes is wrong with him.

"You shall know the truth, and the truth shall make you free." We take the first step in healing by knowing the truth about the body. What is your body? Is it you or is it yours? Are you in your body or outside of your body? In the past, we have thought of our body as that mass of flesh, bone, and skin that we see reflected in the mirror when we stand before it. We have thought of ourselves as living creatures shut up inside a body with a heart, lungs, liver, kidneys, stomach, and other organs to keep it alive; and some kind of a mind to move it where we want it to be.

Let us settle this matter once and for all time. Let us find out just where we are in relation to our body. It is very important that we understand this. Are you in your body, or are you somewhere else? Is the body *you,* or is it *yours?* Have you ever been in your body? If so, how did you get in there? How shall we answer these questions? Let us explore for a moment. Look a t your body and try to find out just where you are located in it. Are you in your head, your throat, your lungs, stomach, legs, arms, or hands?

Hold out your hand and study it. Ask yourself these questions: Is that hand *me* or is it *mine?* Is that arm *me* or is it *mine?* It can't be *me* because I can live without it. Many people lose their arms and legs too, and go right on living. You can cut out all sorts of organs and parts of the body and man goes right on living.

Then where am *I?* In the brains, nerves, solar plexus, or spine?

Go clear through your body, organ by organ, function by function, tissue by tissue, and you will not find a trace of yourself in it.

What is the conclusion? That you have never been inside that body called *you* and that you couldn't get in there even if you tried. What does this prove? That the body is not *you.* But it is yours. It is simply a concept, or form of consciousness—an idea projected by your own thinking and so subject to your own thought about it. You got the idea that you were a material body that in the nature of things gets sick, suffers, and dies through your belief that living implies the need of something to live in. To exist at all, you thought that you had to be in something that you and others could see and feel.

What, then, did you see when you stood before the mirror? You saw your body, but you were not there. Where, then, are you? The answers to these questions are in your surroundings.

Now look at yourself again. What do you see? You see a body called by your name sitting in a chair. The chair is in a room. You are holding this book in your hand. Perhaps there is a table near by and a lamp on it by which you read. Look around at the furniture and other things in this room and then ask yourself these questions: Where are these objects that I cognize with my physical senses? Where are this body, this book, this chair, this lamp? Are they outside of me as they appear to be, or are they inside my consciousness, inside me?

They are inside me.

Why?

Because I am conscious of them. I am conscious of a body, book, room, and chair, and my consciousness of these things is my relation to them.

What does this prove?

It proves that I am consciousness and nothing else.

Carry this truth out into your affairs, and you will see that everything you are or have is your consciousness of it. Your job is your consciousness of it. Your profession is your consciousness of it. Your church is your consciousness of it. Your body is your consciousness of it. Your disease is your consciousness of it. In fact, nothing in your world exists apart from or outside your consciousness.

Do you understand now why the metaphysician says, "Life is a state of consciousness"? Everything that seems to go on in your world, whether good or bad, is not in the world at all but in your consciousness. You are consciousness. Your life is mental and spiritual; it is not physical. The body that you have identified as yourself is not you at all. It is a form (mental concept) in consciousness, subject to your own thoughts and feelings about it.

You may not like the idea that your body is very much like a ventriloquist's dummy and in essence is made of the same fundamental stuff. Think of the ventriloquist as the mind and of the dummy as the body, and you will see why this is true. The antics, activities, and behavior of the dummy are not in the dummy but in the mind of the ventriloquist. The dummy is but a wooden form through which the ventriloquist expresses himself. The dummy may seem very real and human at times; but take the ventriloquist away, and he is nothing but a lump of inanimate matter.

So it is with the dummy called your physical body. Without the mind that animates, thinks, feels, and acts through the body, there is nothing there but $8.75 worth of chemicals and a lump of clay. "That is all tommy rot," you say. "Doesn't the Bible tell us that we are made in the image and likeness of God?" Of course it does. Then how can you posit this idea of the ventriloquist and the dummy? Because the reference to creation in the Bible does not refer to physical image but to the mental and spiritual image. The Real Self, made in God's Image, is Spirit, not matter. Put your physical body in its proper place and see it as a mental concept or form in consciousness.

In higher metaphysics, we seek to demonstrate consciousness, for consciousness is the substance of all forms. It is the substance of everything in our world. In this consciousness, we conceive of our desires as already in complete fulfillment, for in the Absolute there is no time or space. It can only think of desires as already fulfilled. We do not outline the way or channels through which our good will come. We have only to maintain our awareness of the Christ Presence and Principle does the work through us.

In this consciousness, there is no effort to demonstrate or to get things, for Infinite Wisdom, knowing our needs and knowing Itself in us AS US, supplies all these things even before the need appears. We do not treat or parry for jobs or positions because we do not know what job or position is best for us to have. *"Your heavenly Father knoweth that ye have need of all these things* [health, prosperity, peace, joy, security]. It is better to leave the matter to Him. The rule is always this: *"Seek ye first the Kingdom of God* [get the spiritual sense of life] *and all these things shall be added unto you."*

This is not an attitude of passing the buck; It is living by indirection. It is letting the Truth demonstrate Itself; it is realizing that God is always fulfilling Himself in us and in our affairs. To know the Truth that makes us free means that we are not to concern ourselves with the claims and things of the material world, but that we must keep our thought steadfastly on God as the Source, Form, and Substance of all Supply. When the metaphysician says, "My own shall come to me," he means that his own state of consciousness will always demonstrate itself; that is, it will always take form in his experience.

Did Jesus ever refer to Himself as body? Did He ever claim that He was body? Take your concordance and find out for yourself. What did He say in answer to Pilate's question,

"What is truth?" He said, *"I am Truth."* Is truth something that you can see, touch, or taste? Is it something tangible or ponderable? Does it have form? Yet Jesus said, *"I am Truth."*

You can say that, too, but nothing will happen unless you have an awareness of Truth. Declaring Truth does not heal sickness nor establish the Truth of God. It was true before you said it; it did not become true because you said it. What happens when you say, "I am Truth"? Do you change anything by the statement? Not unless you first have the awareness of Truth. Not unless you are the Truth in action. When you know the Truth, you accept the words, *"All that the Father hath is mine."*

"Yet in my flesh shall I see God." Do you believe this? Does your conscious mind grasp it? What does the Bible say? *"His flesh shall be fresher than a child's; he returneth to the days of his youth."* How can this be? How can old, tired, and sick bodies become fresh as a child's? How shall we see God materialized in the flesh? By realizing that we are not confined to a body, by knowing that we have never been in a body.

Have you had a glimpse of the Real Self—the Spiritual Self—as detached from the physical body but controlling it and determining in every respect its health and condition?

The Spiritual Body is perfect in every detail. The material body manifests this perfection when we let it do so, when we live in the consciousness of this perfection. When we meet the shadow of dimming sight with the consciousness of the perfection of the spiritual vision, the false claim is dissolved.

The body is not you; it is yours. You (the Real Self) determine what it manifests. Speak to it with authority. In Isaiah, we find this promise: *"So shall my word be that goeth forth out of my mouth: it shall not return unto me void, but it shall accomplish that which I please, and it shall prosper in the thing whereto I sent it."*

When you have the perspective that the concept of the Spiritual Body gives you, you speak and live in the consciousness of the Absolute — the consciousness of the Unconditioned — the consciousness of God.

Accept this concept of your Real Self now and enter into your inheritance.

Chapter XII
Making an End of Praying

"Now when Solomon had made an end of praying, the fire came down from heaven and consumed the burnt offering and the sacrifices; and the glory of the Lord filled the house [Solomon's consciousness]."

"Now when Solomon had made an end of praying [that is, when he turned everything over to God]," the thing happened. God took over, and the need was met. What is this fire which descends from heaven and sets all things right? It is the Presence of God acting according to faith, filling the cup held up to the Universe, responding to the smallest or greatest need. It is the same fire which Moses saw in the burning bush. It is the Holy Fire of Spirit. It is that power which reveals *"those things which God hath prepared"* that *"eye hath not seen, nor ear heard, neither have entered into the heart of man."*

We do not need to worry as to how God is going to do the seemingly impossible thing for us. He had *"a way"* we *"know not of."* Can we lean on Him instead of on appearances? Can we trust Him? Can we make an end of our prayer so that old beliefs and pictures can be destroyed and new be manifested? Can we believe in one Power instead of two? If our answers to these questions are in the affirmative, our needs are already met. The tears of fear, worry, and struggle are dried up. Where there is infection, it is burned out. Where there is bitterness, it is consumed. Where there is opposition, it is dissolved. The ugly manifestation that has caused our grief is, in the twinkling of an eye, destroyed. Our whole consciousness is filled with the glory of the Lord. We are confident and certain of the outcome of our prayer. The invisible fire released through the single eye has made all things new.

When we make *"an end of praying,"* we have accepted what is embodied in the prayer and, without any further anxiety, expectantly await its materialization.

Protracted praying is an open acknowledgement of doubt and mistrust. When we keep repeating a treatment, we only widen the gap between us and the object of our prayer. "But," you say, "we are told to *'Pray without ceasing.'* " Praying without ceasing means carrying faith into action; it is not a repetitive mouthing of words. It is a consistent effort to think right. It is constantly thanking God for the work that has already been done. It is keeping the eye single and unwavering in spite of every unfavorable appearance. It is keeping faith resolutely fixed during the crucial period of gestation on the wish fulfilled. In modern terminology, we would probably say that this is the "follow up" of the verbal prayer.

To continue praying, treating, or affirming is evidence that we do not have faith in our prayer. The Law says, *"Whatsoever things ye desire, when ye pray, BELIEVE that ye have received them, and ye shall have them."* The prayer that gets results is the prayer of acceptance. It is the only form of prayer that precludes doubt. Habakkuk says, *"For the vision has its own appointed hour. It is ripening. It will flower. If it be long then wait, for it is sure, and it will not be late."* St. James said, *"Ye ask and receive not because ye ask amiss."*

Do you remember the warning Jesus sounded, *"When ye pray use not vain repetitions as the heathen do; for they think they shall be heard for their much speaking. Be not ye therefore like unto them,*

---

* Moffat translation of the Bible.

for your Heavenly Father knoweth what things ye have need of before ye ask Him"?

The thing that we do not realize when we are distraught is that vain repetitions and much speaking in prayer not only deepen belief in the problem but keep it alive. The prayer of faith is the prayer of acceptance. Solomon made *"an end of praying"* because he accepted the fact that God would answer his prayer.

Probably the greatest scourge of metaphysical students is the divided mind, which is the only devil there is. Trying to see spiritually, trying to think straight, trying to pray constantly, and trying to know the truth while the conscious mind grapples with contradictory evidence pull you in two directions at the same time.

A loved one is desperately ill. Appearances are alarming. The condition goes up and down like the thermometer on the outside of your house. The doctors say that they have done all they can. A friend is in deep trouble, and there is no apparent way out of it. A mortgage is about to be foreclosed, and there is no money in sight. You have prayed night and day and your treatments seem to fall on deaf ears. You ask, " *'Is there no balm in Gilead, is there no physician there?'* Is there no end to these blood transfusions, antibiotics, hypos, serums, pills, and medications, to these threats, menaces, intimidations? Why aren't my prayers answered? Why doesn't God hear my please?"

There is one answer: You have prayed but you have not made an end of praying. Your spiritual vision is defective; you are still seeing double. You are looking in two directions at the same time, one straightforward and righteous, and the other distorted and defeating. Double-mindedness keeps you in a state of frustration and confusion by denying and scattering the good which you seek.

Jesus said, *"The lamp of thy body is thine eye; when thine eye is single, thy whole body is also full of light, but when it is evil* [divided between appearances and Reality], *thy body also is full of darkness."** The cure for double-mindedness is an increase of faith; it is brought about by praying, *"nothing wavering,"* and releasing the prayer and condition to God. St. James says: *"If any of you lack wisdom, let him ask of God, that giveth to all men liberally and upbraideth not; and it shall be given him. But let him ask in faith nothing wavering; for he that wavereth is like the sea driven with the wind and tossed. For let not that man think that he shall receive anything of the Lord. A double-minded man is unstable in all his ways."*

The antidote for double-mindedness is not found in the occulist's office nor in the apothecary's shop; it is stated in the Bible. *"Look unto Me all ye ends of the earth and be ye saved."* Since double-mindedness is the result of dividing attention between good and evil, the cure for it is to concentrate upon the good by practicing the Presence of God without ceasing.

Basically, the cause of double-mindedness is lack of faith. The answer to the sink-or-swim prayer born in a moment of desperation is often long delayed because of the habitual tendency to worry. When the mountains suddenly tumble in on us, when the skies grow heavy and black and the hurricane blows in our faces, we tend to lose control of our thoughts and emotions and to give the weight of our mind to the problem instead of to God. In a moment of fleeting panic, caused by the breaking-up of a familiar pattern, we seem to be more

---

* American Standard Version of the Bible.

impressed by the power of evil which is evidenced by sense than by the power of Good which is known of the spirit. But the channels can be kept open for the good to get to us by the realization that no situation is hopeless.

If your are meeting a crisis, suffering a moment of panic, facing an overwhelming loss, and seeing only the difficulty, sit down with this thought and relax yourself into God's Presence, "No situation is hopeless." Hold your mind in a state of quietude and peace until you are able to see your situation clearly. *"Be still and know that I am God."* Be so still that the surface of your mind is like a placid pool without a ripple.

"Be still and know that I am God" is another way of saying *"Let this Mind be in you which was also in Christ Jesus."* Jesus, as you know, often affirmed his unity with God. He said, *"I and the Father are one"* and *"The Father that dwelleth in me, He doeth the works."*

To have the Mind *"which was also in Christ Jesus,"* we must first get calm. We need confidence and assurance, but we cannot have them until we share God's quietness. Instead of agonizing in prayer and struggling with God, we must fix our spiritual gaze so steadfastly upon the Truth of God's spiritual creation that the troublesome thoughts become completely obliterated from our minds. We cannot work our problems out metaphysically so long as our attention is divided between conditions and Reality. *"Choose ye this day whom ye will serve."*

The majesty of calmness, the assurance of detachment, the power of quietness — what balm these are to the troubled soul! This is the state of mind St. Paul referred to when he said, *"None of these things move me,"* and by *"none,"* he meant the evidence of the material senses. Don't get distraught. Don't get upset.

Keep peaceful. Remain composed, and the assurance you are seeking will come. Hold your problem in thought, knowing that there is an answer already prepared, and say to yourself, *"God does not bring to birth and then not bring forth."* Say it until your mind ceases to be troubled. The child (the answer to your prayer) will be born when the conflict in your mind stops. If you can remain calm, imperturbable, and steadfast in the midst of trouble, you will rise victoriously over it.

When Jesus tells us to *"Consider the lilies of the field,"* He is not inviting us to smell their perfume or to look at their beauty but to consider *"how they grow."* They let the power operate through them. *"They toil not, neither do they spin."* If we are too busy to consider the lilies, we shall never learn the secret of answered prayer.

There is an oak in the acorn, a flower in the seed a chicken in the egg. How shall we get them out into the open? *By leaving them to God.*

According to the New Testament, the two basic factors in successful prayer are faith and works, but *"Faith without works is dead."* It is not enough to pray. We must also act as if the prayer were true. We must carry our faith into action. Faith is the magnet that materializes our good, and work is the unfaltering trust that enables us to face our vicissitudes in the confident knowledge that if we do our part faithfully, God will do His. The time and effort spent in prayer make no difference unless we carry our faith into action. If we return to our daily tasks after prayer in the fearful and negative state of mind which we brought to it, the condition will remain unchanged. We have dwelt so long in the doubts and apprehensions of the conscious thinking, that it takes heroic effort to lift the mind into a positive conception of perfection and truth and hold it there. "What if *this* should happen or *that* should occur," "Maybe the diagnosis is wrong," "Perhaps the deal will fall through," "Suppose *this* and suppose *that*" — just a few words like these are all that is needed for our faith to evaporate into thin air like a puff of smoke.

The imagination is no help at this moment unless it is utilized to visualize Truth in action, to see mentally the good for which the prayer is made. The psychologist tells us that the will obeys the imagination because the imaging power is stronger than will power. It is the image in the mind that gives form and content to purpose. If we would reach a point of absolute acceptance in our prayers, the imagination must be God-centered.

Why did Jesus lay so much emphasis upon prayer? Because prayer is the great conditioner of the mind and soul. By our prayer, we condition ourselves to receive the great things God can do through us.

Do you believe that God can do all things? Do you believe that there is nothing impossible to God? Do you believe that He is the source of supply? Do you believe that He can dissolve that lump? Do you believe that He can establish perfect right action in that heart? Certainly He can, but not until you have arrived at the point of acceptance. First, you must believe that you already have what you have asked for, and you must stop taking thought about it. Second, you must make an end of the prayer. You must assume that *"It is done."* Every prayer and affirmation must be made in the attitude of acceptance. Prayer is not begging or petitioning God but releasing the Power within.

Effective prayer depends not upon words or forms but upon realization of our oneness or unity with God. When the mind is unified with God, the prayer is no longer divided between health and disease, plenty and lack, courage and fear, peace and discord but is so filled with God's Presence that there is no room for anything else.

One essential in a successful treatment or prayer is to eliminate the personal, to refuse to dwell on shortcomings and mistakes, to forgive and forget the past.

Forgiveness works in two ways. Through it, we not only free others, we free ourselves, too. It is a reciprocal process. Before the entry into Jerusalem, Jesus said, *"When ye stand praying, forgive, if ye have aught against any man: that your Father also which is in heaven may forgive you your trespasses."* That there is no limit to the extent we are called upon to exercise forgiveness is evidenced by His answer to Peter's question, *"How oft shall my brother sin against me and I forgive him? till seven times?"* You recall His words, *"I say not unto thee, Until seven times: but Until seventy times seven."* Then there are the promises, *"For if ye forgive men their trespasses, your Heavenly Father will also forgive you,"* and *"Judge not, and ye shall not be judged: condemn not, and ye shall not be condemned: forgive, and ye shall be forgiven."*

Daily we say the words, *"Forgive us our debts as we forgive our debtors,"* but all too often they form on the lips and have no place nor power in the mind and heart. We sometimes find it easier to forgive a large offense than a small one. All too often we fail to realize that among our debtors may be those against whom we have resentment for slight causes, grudges for unfulfilled promises, or criticism for failing to live up to our standards. These, too, must be forgiven.

Only by forgiveness do we make it possible for God to do His mighty works through us. If Divine Power is to operate, the channel must be made by eliminating all animosity, antagonism, bitterness, and condemnation.

We can, then, make our prayers more effective by remembering to do these things:

1. Hold fast to the intention or idea embodied in the prayer.

2. Keep attention pin-pointed on God's perfection and the good sought.

3. Refuse any compromise with evil.

4. Refuse to admit any contrary evidence.

5. Refuse to judge according to appearances.

6. Follow faith into action. Keep it moving toward desire.

7. Stand *"having done all* [that is, having released the desire and its accomplishment whole-heartedly to God]."

In the end, however, it is not the prayer that brings the fulfillment of our desires; it is not the words we use that effect the result. The answer comes out of a deep-rooted conviction, a unified state of mind, and a refusal to compromise our intention in any way. When we know with our hearts and minds that God is the only Power in the Universe, we can never fall victim to doubt, fear, or worry. We can pray the prayer of faith and thanksgiving and confidently make an *"end of praying."*

Raisa - Mystic Alchemist

Energy Healing, Chakra Alignment, Sacred Geometry, Sound Healing

Tammy:

I was blessed with a healing session by Raisa last week. She felt like a friend and like-minded gentle soul with comforting Mother Mary essence pouring through her words. Raisa was so in-tuned to my blocks and traumas held within my field. She used her connection to ascended masters I've resonated with such as Yeshua, Mother Mary, Mary Magdalene, Lady Vesta & Amethyst and archangels Metatron, Michael and others to help clear these.

I was able to address childhood trauma situations to flip the stuck energy I've held onto over the years. She also picked up on a few traumatic past-life scenes that have affected my current life. I am an intuitive energy healer who truly felt the shift and healing within. I now feel so much lighter and have clarity regarding my path.

So much love and gratitude to you both, Raisa and Barry for presenting her to my world! (More Testimonials on following Pages)

Contact Raisa to book an Energy Healing
or Chakra Alignment session:
www.RaisinYourIsness.com
raisinyourisness@hotmail.com

Shannon:

This BEAUTIFUL sister...our Raisa... is a treasure beyond compare! After my experience in my personal session with Raisa... the ABSOLUTE confirmation I received, that could ONLY be confirmed by HER mind you... this session solidified EVERYTHING for me. I KNOW that this sister... she is a formidable, magnificent & IRREPLACEABLE component in this Earth plane story we all are invested in! IF YOU ARE DRAWN TO HER FOLLOW YOUR HEART

No other can do what SHE is gifted to do for YOU... YES YOU!

I LOVE YOU dear sister! I am forever grateful for what only you could do and DID for me! I would have happily paid any price for what you gave me! I URGE YOU ALL to schedule a session with this beloved one!

P.S. thank you Barry for sharing her with us all!

∞

Natasha:

I would like to thank Barry for introducing us to Raisa. I have had 2 consultations with her in the last month and I am in total awe of what transpired. Raisa is such a beautiful caring soul! She connected with me as though she has known me forever. Her love and dedication in assisting others is so touching. I had an amazing experience and some profound healing. I received a message from Jeshua which brought tears to my eyes. I could feel the LOVE in the message that was given to me and I will remember and cherish His message forever. Raisa has really helped me in confronting fears, trauma and past life karma. I have found the reason for my skin problems which I never would have thought it'd be possible. It is amazing what guilt and shame from past lives can actually do to your body. Her healing and that from our Angelic beings has really made a huge difference in my life. I can feel it in my energy. Raisa has a lovely sense of humour, always reminding you not to take life and yourself so seriously. I really feel like a heavy weight has been lifted off my soul. Thank you so much! Much Love!

∞

Ariel:

Raisa... Divine Raisa... You are a Treasure to this Life, and I thank All That Is, and this also Treasured YT channel for the priceless blessing which was our session this AM. Every moment of the session was a fractal explosion of wonderful intuitive & divinely guided perfection. I honor your sincere, caring, graceful, playful, soothing, encouraging, transformational, empowering, and so beautiful demonstration / embodiment of Goddess energy and presence. I am so honored & thankful to have been guided to You. To have invested in the patience, time, energy, and resources to share sacred healing and uplifting time with You. I will remember the session Always. And I will look forward to any and all ways our Creator deems it harmonious to connect again. I could go on and on and on, so please accept my parting acknowledgment of your blessing to this realm, my Heart & Spirt, my Life, and the Lives of all those who may be positively impacted via your assistance. Blessings, and Gratitude, a thousand times over and over again. Namaste... Namaste... Namaste...

∞

B.G.

I have just finished a healing session with Raisa. The experience was remarkable! I am still buzzing! I heard about her from this channel, so thank you deeply Barry!

Raisa is so lovely to talk to, and intuitively guided, knows how to get to the hidden roots of our issues. She calls upon ascended masters, archangels and such to do deep energetic clearing and healing work. It was like being guided through the deep layers of myself, releasing the things that don't serve me and filling every cell with light. I purged, and I absorbed new energy, and came out feeling uplifted and renewed. Raisa helped me to find things in myself that I had been cut off from, and to heal wounds I had tried to bury. She has also given me helpful ideas to continue to improve things my life.

I am so blessed to have found Raisa, and ever grateful for the healing work she has done. She is as authentic as they come. Truly an earth angel! Thank you, thank you, thank you!

▶ YouTube

YouTube Channels of Interest:

Giving Voice to the Wisdom of the Ages

Over 5,000 audios, hundreds of
Spiritual and Metaphysical
audio books including
Robert A Russell, Dr Murdo MacDonald Bayne,
Napoleon Hill, Jeshua, Kryon and many more.

I AM Meditations and Affirmations

Hundreds of I AM Meditations,
Daily affirmations and more.

Raisin' Your Isness

Metaphysical Musings, Channelings,
Sound Healing Songs